Grammar Booster 1
Megan Roderick

Acknowledgements

Special thanks to Sarah Bideleux for preparing the grammar theory.

Illustrated by Panagiotis Angeletakis

© 2012 National Geographic Learning, as part of Cengage Learning

ISBN: 978-960-403-098-9 Student's Book

ISBN: 978-960-403-097-2 Teacher's Book

National Geographic Learning
Cheriton House, North Way, Andover, Hampshire, SP10 5BE
United Kingdom

Cengage Learning is a leading provider of customized learning solutions with office locations around the globe, including Singapore, the United Kingdom, Australia, Mexico, Brazil and Japan. Locate your local office at:
international.cengage.com/region

Cengage Learning products are represented in Canada by Nelson Education, Ltd.

Visit National Geographic Learning online at **ngl.cengage.com**

Visit our corporate website at **www.cengage.com**

Printed in the United Kingdom by Lightning Source
Print Number: 09   Print Year: 2017

Contents

Subject Pronouns & Present Simple: To Be

Hi, Tonic!

Good morning, Jim.

Am I big and strong, Tonic?

Yes, you are, Jim.

Am I clever, Tonic?

Yes, you are, Jim.

He isn't very clever, but he's my friend.

Subject Pronouns

Singular	Plural
I	we
you	you
he	they
she	
it	

Subject pronouns show who or what something does or is.
I am happy today.

We use *it* for things or animals. But if the animal is our pet, we often use *he* or *she*.
Look at the dog. It's very big.
I love my dog. He's wonderful.

We use *you* for the singular and the plural.
You are a good friend, David.
You are good friends, John and Sarah.

We use *they* for a lot of people, animals or things.
Where are the boys? They're in the park.
Are dogs clever? Yes, they are.
Where are the pens? They're on the table.

1 Write the Subject Pronouns.

Eg   *Uncle John*   ......*he*......

1   Jim   ....

2   the cat   ....

3   Lucy   ....

4   my mother   ....

5   Mum and Dad   ....

6   my friend and I ....

7   the television ....

8   the books   ....

Present Simple: To Be

Affirmative	Negative	Question
I am (I'm)	I am not (I'm not)	Am I?
you are (you're)	you are not (you aren't)	Are you?
he is (he's)	he is not (he isn't)	Is he?
she is (she's)	she is not (she isn't)	Is she?
it is (it's)	it is not (it isn't)	Is it?
we are (we're)	we are not (we aren't)	Are we?
you are (you're)	you are not (you aren't)	Are you?
they are (they're)	they are not (they aren't)	Are they?

Short answers

Yes, I am.	No, I'm not.
Yes, you are.	No, you aren't.
Yes, he is.	No, he isn't.
Yes, she is.	No, she isn't.
Yes, it is.	No, it isn't.
Yes, we are.	No, we aren't.
Yes, you are.	No, you aren't.
Yes, they are.	No, they aren't.

We use *to be* to talk about someone's job, nationality, relationship or his or her name.
He is a doctor.   *She is my sister.*
We are Italian.   *I am Helen.*

We also use *to be* to describe people and things.
The sea is blue.
We are happy.

In everyday English, we use the short form.
Hi. I'm Susan.

We use *to be* with subject pronouns (*I, you, he,* etc) and other words.
He is sad.
The ball is green and red.

THINK ABOUT IT!

*In English there is no difference between **you** singular and **you** plural.*

2 Complete the sentences with the Present Simple of **to be**.

Eg I .... am .... very thirsty. ✓

1 He .... happy today. ✗
2 You .... a good friend. ✓
3 I .... hungry. ✗
4 The flowers in the garden .... very pretty. ✓
5 The television .... in the sitting room. ✗
6 The sea .... near our house. ✓
7 The books .... on the chair. ✗
8 Jim and Tonic .... friends. ✓

3 Choose the correct answer.

Eg Are she / ⟨they⟩ happy?

1 I / We am a good student.
2 Is you / he clever?
3 We / She are tired.
4 He / I is at school.
5 They / She are English.
6 Is she / they in the bedroom?
7 We / He aren't in the garden.
8 She / I isn't in the kitchen.

5

4 Complete the questions with **am**, **are** or **is** and write answers.

THINK ABOUT IT!

Affirmative short answers do not use the short form of **to be**.

Eg ....*Is*.......... it Monday today? ✓
.........*Yes, it is*.......... .

1 .... you at home now? ✓
....

2 .... the clothes on the bed? ✗
....

3 .... the computer on the desk? ✓
....

4 .... I clever? ✓
....

5 .... breakfast ready? ✗
....

6 .... she outside the door? ✓
....

7 .... we at the right house? ✓
....

8 .... the cats in the basket? ✗
....

Present Simple: To Be, negative questions

Negative questions

Aren't I?
Aren't you?
Isn't he?
Isn't she?
Isn't it?
Aren't we?
Aren't you?
Aren't they?

We use negative questions when we expect the answer: 'Yes'.
Isn't it hot today?
Yes, it is. It's very hot.

5 Complete the questions with **aren't** or **isn't**.

Eg ....*Isn't*.......... it a nice day today!
1 .... I clever?
2 .... she ready?
3 .... he at work today?
4 .... the puppies in the basket?
5 .... they angry about the broken window?
6 .... the chocolate cake good?
7 .... you tired after your walk?
8 .... the teacher happy with your work?

6 Rewrite the sentences with Subject Pronouns.

Eg Are <u>the children</u> in the garden?
Are they in the garden?

1 <u>The restaurant</u> is next to the sea.
....

2 <u>Peter</u> isn't on the bus.
....

3 Isn't <u>the actress</u> good?
....

4 <u>My family and I</u> are very happy to see you.
....

5 Is <u>the doctor</u> on the phone?
....

6 <u>Mum and Dad</u> aren't in the kitchen.
....

7 Write sentences or questions with **to be**.

Eg *he / be / very strong*
..... *He is very strong.* ....

1 you / be / tired / today / ?

....

2 the sea / be / very warm

....

3 I / not be / tall

....

4 the books / be / on her desk

....

5 our friends / not be / at home at the moment

....

6 you / be / ready / for lunch / ?

....

7 Tonic / be / a nice dog

....

8 she / be / at the gym now

....

8 Complete the text with **is, isn't, are** or **aren't**.

(Eg) .... *Is* .... Jim happy today? Yes, he (1) .... It (2) .... a beautiful day. The sky (3) .... cloudy. It (4) .... blue. Jim (5) .... at work. He (6) .... in the park giving bread to the ducks. The ducks (7) .... hungry! Tonic (8) .... with Jim. He (9) .... at home. Jim's friends (10) .... at the park. They (11) .... at work!

Pairwork

Work with a partner. Take turns to ask and answer the following questions:

- Is it sunny today?
- Are you at school now?
- Is your mum at home now?
- Are your books heavy?
- Is your best friend with you now?

- Are you hungry?
- Are you thirsty?
- Is it hot outside?
- Is it lunchtime?
- Is this book easy?

Writing

Write in your diary.
Think about:

- where you are now.
- what the weather is like.
- where the other members of your family are.

....
....
....
....
....
....
....
....
....
....

Articles, Regular & Irregular Plurals

The Indefinite Article

a	an
a book	an ant
a girl	an egg
a house	an island
a garden	an owl
a bone	an umbrella
a uniform	an hour
a yellow ball	an interesting lesson
a green apple	an adventure story
a horrible day	an orange bag

We use the indefinite articles *a* and *an* with singular nouns.
a girl　　　　*an egg*

We use *a* before a consonant *(b, c, d, f, g, h, j, k, l, m, n, p, q, r, s, t, v, w, x, y, z)* and *an* before a vowel *(a, e, i, o, u).*
an apple　　　　*a film*

Sometimes there is an adjective before the noun. When the adjective begins with a consonant, we use *a*. When it begins with a vowel, we use *an*.
a green apple　　　　*an interesting film*

We use *a* or *an* to talk about one person, animal or thing in general. (We don't use *a* or *an* to talk about someone or something specific.)
A bag is on the table.　　　*There's a man outside.*

Notes
Be careful! Some words begin with *h* or *u*. When the word begins with a consonant sound, we use *a*. When the word begins with a vowel sound, we use *an*.
an hour, an umbrella, an uncle
a hat, a hospital, a hotel, a unit, a university, a uniform

1 Write **a** or **an**.

Eg ....an....... apple
1 .... island
2 .... zoo
3 .... clock
4 .... octopus
5 .... kite
6 .... doctor
7 .... Indian
8 .... hotel
9 .... hour
10 .... elephant

2 Write **a** or **an**.

Eg ....a....... clever boy
1 .... nice girl
2 .... exciting film
3 .... interesting book
4 .... happy child
5 .... yellow T-shirt
6 .... red umbrella
7 .... awful day
8 .... big house
9 .... orange notebook
10 .... useful lesson

The Definite Article

the

The moon is white.
The Atlantic Ocean is very big.
The green books are on the table.

We use the definite article *the*:

- to talk about specific people, things or animals (singular or plural).
  The boy in the red T-shirt is outside.
  The blue trousers are on the bed.

- to talk about something that is unique.
  Look at the sky. It's so blue!

- with the names of mountain ranges (the Himalayas), oceans (the Pacific Ocean) and seas (the Black Sea), rivers (the Thames) and deserts (the Sahara Desert).

- with musical instruments.
  He plays the guitar.

We don't use *the*:

- with people's names.
  Paul and David are best friends.

- with the names of countries. (But we say: the United States, the Netherlands, etc.)
  China is an interesting country.

- with subjects, games or sports.
  History is my favourite subject.
  Cluedo is a great game!
  She plays basketball.

- when the noun is plural and we are talking about people, animals or things in general.
  I like films.
  Elephants are very large animals.

3 Complete the sentences with **a**, **an** or **the**.

Eg *There's ....a....... tree in ...the....... garden and there is ....a....... ball under ...the....... tree.*

1 There's .... book on the table. .... book is interesting.

2 There is .... table in my room. On .... table, there is .... bowl.
There is .... apple in .... bowl.

3 London is .... very big city. In .... city there are millions of people.
.... people of London are great!

4 Look! There's .... man in .... street. .... man has got .... umbrella.
.... umbrella is red and white.

9

4 Complete the sentences with **the** or **–**.

Eg   *The* Nile is in Africa.

1   My cousins are on a skiing holiday in .... Alps.
2   I like .... history.
3   She lives in .... USA.
4   My cousin plays .... drums.

5   .... Nile is a long river.
6   .... sun is very hot today.
7   A lot of tourists go to .... Paris to see the Eiffel Tower.
8   Big Ben is in .... London.

Regular Plurals

Singular	Plural
pencil	pencils
bus	buses
dress	dresses
brush	brushes
watch	watches
fox	foxes
photo	photos
tomato	tomatoes
wife	wives
leaf	leaves
party	parties
boy	boys

Irregular Plurals

Singular	Plural
child	children
man	men
woman	women
person	people
foot	feet
tooth	teeth
mouse	mice
sheep	sheep
deer	deer
goose	geese
ox	oxen

We usually make a noun plural by adding -s.

chair   ➡   chairs
table   ➡   tables

We add -es to words that end in -s, -ss, -sh, -ch and -x.

dress   ➡   dresses
fox   ➡   foxes

When a word ends in a consonant and -y, we take off the -y and add -ies.

baby   ➡   babies

When a word ends in a vowel and -y, we just add -s.

key   ➡   keys
birthday   ➡   birthdays

We usually add -s to words that end in -o. Sometimes we add -es.

piano   ➡   pianos
photo   ➡   photos
tomato   ➡   tomatoes
potato   ➡   potatoes

When a word ends in -f or -fe, we usually take off the -f or -fe and add -ves. But we just add -s to the words *giraffe* and *roof*.

wife   ➡   wives
half   ➡   halves
giraffe   ➡   giraffes
roof   ➡   roofs

Irregular plurals do not follow any rules. You must learn them.

5 Write the plurals.

Eg *day* ....*days*.....................

1 knife ....

2 piano ....

3 table ....

4 tomato ....

5 sandwich ....

6 country ....

7 box ....

8 dish ....

9 address ....

10 plane ....

THINK ABOUT IT!

*We say **one** instead of **an** when we are counting.*

6 Write the plurals.

Eg *ox* ....*oxen*.....................

1 sheep ....

2 mouse ....

3 man ....

4 tooth ....

5 goose ....

6 person ....

7 child ....

8 foot ....

9 woman ....

10 deer ....

7 Complete the sentences with the plural of the words in brackets.

Eg *He's got two hundred* ....*books*.....................*! (book)*

1 Six .... are in the field. (sheep)

2 Ten .... are on the bus. (person)

3 Two .... are in the street. (man)

4 Three .... are playing computer games. (boy)

5 A lot of .... are in the playground. (child)

6 He's got big .... (foot)

7 Her .... are very white. (tooth)

8 The .... are ready now. (pizza)

9 There are four .... on the table. (glass)

10 We've got two .... for the weekend. (video)

8 Find ten plural words.

B	O	F	P	S	E	P	E	N	S	T	O	R
A	B	O	X	E	S	A	G	D	O	C	X	M
Z	R	X	I	O	P	R	H	O	U	S	E	S
B	U	E	L	A	T	T	N	A	M	M	S	T
T	S	S	S	E	O	I	H	S	M	E	N	E
C	H	I	L	D	R	E	N	T	W	W	V	E
Z	E	Y	C	K	X	S	O	K	R	R	A	T
U	S	L	L	A	D	I	E	S	F	F	R	H
A	S	T	R	A	W	B	E	R	R	I	E	S

Writing

Write a list of the things in your room.

....

....

....

....

....

....

....

....

....

....

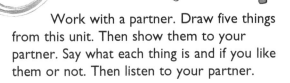

Pairwork

Work with a partner. Draw five things from this unit. Then show them to your partner. Say what each thing is and if you like them or not. Then listen to your partner.

11

Prepositions of Place
& There Is / There Are

Prepositions of Place

at	in	next to
behind	in front of	on
between	near	under

We use prepositions of place to show where something or someone is located. The most common prepositions of place are:

- at;
  She is at her house in the country.

- behind;
  They live behind the school.

- between;
  The bank is between the post office and the supermarket.

- in;
  The present is in the bag.

- in front of;
  The blackboard is in front of the students.

- near;
  We live near the hospital.

- next to;
  The bed is next to the window.

- on;
  The cat is on the chair.

- under;
  The umbrella is under the chair.

Complete the sentences with the words in the box.

behind   in   near   on
between   in front of   next to   under

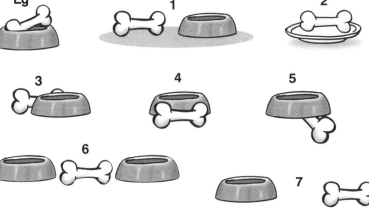

Eg   *The bone is ....in........... the bowl.*

1   The bone is .... the bowl.

2   The bone is .... the plate.

3   The bone is .... the bowl.

4   The bone is .... the bowl.

5   The bone is .... the bowl.

6   The bone is .... two bowls.

7   The bone is .... the bowl.

On, In, At

There are some useful phrases with prepositions of place.

on
on the plane/train/bus
on the left/right
on the wall

in
in bed
in hospital
in a car
in the middle
in an armchair

at
at school
at work
at home
at the top
at the bottom

Find the mistakes and write the sentences correctly.

Eg   *Dad isn't in work today.*
        Dad isn't at work today.

1   There is a painting in the wall.

....

2   They are in home today.

....

3   There are five people at the car.

....

4   The house at is the right.

....

5   Grandma sits on her armchair.

....

6   The children are at their bikes now.

....

7   The table is on the middle of the sitting room.

....

8   There are strange animals in the bottom of the sea.

....

There Is / There are

Affirmative	Negative	Question
there is (there's) there are	there is not (there isn't) there are not (there aren't)	Is there ...? Are there ...?

Short answers

Yes, there is. Yes, there are.	No, there isn't. No, there aren't.

We use *there is* and *there are* to talk or ask about what exists when we are describing something in the present.
There is a baby in the garden.
There are two people in the car.
There aren't any big houses here.
Are there two people in the photograph?

3 Choose the correct answer.

Eg   There is / There are two pencils on the desk.

1   *There is / There are* hundreds of cars on the roads.
2   *There is / There are* a post office in the village.
3   *There is / There are* two books on the chair.
4   *There is / There are* elephants at the zoo.
5   *There is / There are* a baby in the family.
6   *There is / There are* a bike in front of the house.
7   *There is / There are* a dog near the school.
8   *There is / There are* three children in the classroom.

4 Write answers.

Eg   *Is there a ball on the chair?* ✓
.............Yes, there is...........

1   Is there a book on the desk? ✗
....

2   Are there sweets in the bowl? ✓
....

3   Are there people in the school? ✗
....

4   Is there ice cream in the freezer? ✓
....

5   Is there a telephone in the hall? ✗
....

6   Is there a computer on the table? ✓
....

7   Are there flowers in the garden? ✓
....

8   Is there a bone in the garden? ✗
....

5

Look at the picture on page 12. Write sentences with **There is** or **There are** and Prepositions of Place.

Eg *(trees)* *There are trees in the garden.*

1 (ball) ....
....

2 (flowers) ....
....

3 (birds) ....
....

4 (book) ....
....

5 (plane) ....
....

6 (umbrella) ....
....

6

Write questions.

Eg *bag / on / desk?*
Is there a bag on the desk?

1 pencil / in / pencil case?
....

2 cat / next to / window?
....

3 cafés / near / sea?
....

4 flowers / in / vase?
....

5 playground / in front of / school?
....
....

7

Complete the text with the words in the box.

behind	between	in	is
middle	next	on	there (x2)

Jim's bedroom

(Eg) ....*In*............ Jim's bedroom
(1) .... are lots of things. In the
(2) .... of the room, there
(3) .... a big bed. (4) ....
the wall (5) .... is a poster of
Superman. Near the window, there is a table
and a chair. (6) .... to the table is
a bookcase. (7) .... the bookcase
and the door there is a big cupboard with
Jim's clothes. Jim's umbrella is (8) ....
the door. What's your bedroom like?

Pairwork

Work with a partner. Take turns to ask and answer about your bedroom or office.

Writing

Write a letter to a friend. Describe your bedroom using *there is* and *there are* and as many different prepositions as you can.

Dear .... ,
....
....
....
....
....
....
....
Your friend,
....

Have Got

What a great day, Tonic!

Oh dear, I haven't got my key, Tonic. Have you got a key?

I've got my key in a special hiding place. Here you are, Jim!

Well done, Tonic! You're brilliant!

Have got

Affirmative	Negative	Question
I have (I've) got	I have not (haven't) got	Have I got?
you have (you've) got	you have not (haven't) got	Have you got?
he has (he's) got	he has not (hasn't) got	Has he got?
she has (she's) got	she has not (hasn't) got	Has she got?
it has (it's) got	it has not (hasn't) got	Has it got?
we have (we've) got	we have not (haven't) got	Have we got?
you have (you've) got	you have not (haven't) got	Have you got?
they have (they've) got	they have not (haven't) got	Have they got?

Short answers

Yes, I have.	No, I haven't.
Yes, you have.	No, you haven't.
Yes, he has.	No, he hasn't.
Yes, she has.	No, she hasn't.
Yes, it has.	No, it hasn't.
Yes, we have.	No, we haven't.
Yes, you have.	No, you haven't.
Yes, they have.	No, they haven't.

We use *have got*:

- to show that something belongs to someone.
  They've got a new camera.

- to describe a person, thing or animal.
  She hasn't got brown hair.
  The house has got a blue door.

- to talk about a health problem.
  I've got toothache.

1 Complete the sentences with the short form of **have got**.

Eg   I ......*'ve got*...... a big dog.

1   You .... lots of rings on your fingers.
2   They .... a house in the country.
3   He .... a good job.
4   She .... two brothers.
5   I .... bad toothache.
6   We .... two goldfish.
7   They .... a small garden.
8   My bedroom .... a large window.

2 Complete the sentences with the negative form of **have got**.

Eg   They ......*haven't got*...... a big flat.

1   She .... a pet.
2   The house .... a big balcony.
3   I .... a black and yellow pen.
4   We .... a house by the sea.
5   Brian .... a car.
6   You .... time for this.
7   She .... blue eyes; she's got green eyes.
8   I .... long hair.

3 Complete the questions with **have got** and the words in brackets.

Eg   (you) ......*Have you got*...... any CDs?

1   (the baby) .... dark hair?
2   (you) .... good friends at school?
3   (I) .... a dirty face?
4   (Martha) .... a headache?
5   (he) .... a motorbike?
6   (they) .... tickets for the concert?
7   (the dog) .... a bone?
8   (village) .... a post office?

THINK ABOUT IT!

In questions, we cannot use the short form.

4 Answer the questions. Give extra information if you can.

Eg   *Have you got brown eyes?*
     No, I haven't. I've got green eyes.
     ....

1   Have you got a CD player?
     ....

2   Have you got short hair?
     ....

3   Have you got a headache?
     ....

4   Have you got brothers and sisters?
     ....

5   Have you got a bike?
     ....

6   Have you got a good job?
     ....

Put the words and phrases in the correct part of the chart.
Then write questions and answers about Jim and Tonic.

THINK ABOUT IT!

*If we want to use the short form of **have got** after a name, we put 's (**has**) after the name.*

a black nose   a nice house   a red coat   a tail
big muscles   fair hair   four legs   Grammarman clothes
ten bones   white fur

Jim's got ...	Tonic's got ...
a nice house	*a black nose*

Eg   *Tonic / a nice house?*
...*Has Tonic got a nice house?*...
...*No, he hasn't. Jim's got a nice house.*...

1   Jim / four legs?
....
....

2   Jim / white fur?
....
....

3   Tonic / ten bones?
....
....

4   Jim / Grammarman clothes?
....
....

5   Tonic / fair hair?
....
....

6   Tonic / a tail?
....
....

7   Jim / a black nose?
....
....

8   Tonic / a red coat?
....
....

Write the words in the correct order.

Eg   *got / hair / you / have / dark / ?*
...*Have you got dark hair?*...

1   has / cat / she / a / white / got
....

2   hasn't / red / he / jacket / got / a
....

3   a piece of cake / got / have / you / ?
....

4   four / they / got / children / haven't
....

5   Jim / white / got / has / Porsche / a / ?
....

6   I / sore finger / got / a / have
....

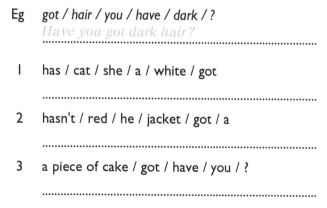

18

7 Rewrite the sentences using the full form.

Eg It's a hot day.
    It is a hot day.

1 Tonic's a clever dog.
   ....

2 Tonic's got a lot of bones.
   ....

3 The boy's in the classroom.
   ....

4 There's a strange person outside.
   ....

THINK ABOUT IT!

She's a tall girl. = She is a tall girl.
She's got a tall sister. = She has got a tall sister.

5 Look at the cake! It's got cherries on it!
   ....

6 She's got a headache.
   ....

7 He's my best friend.
   ....

8 Mary's got two brothers and a sister.
   ....

8 Complete the text with **have got**.

My name's Sandra. I (Eg) ....*have got*........ (✓) a brother and a sister. My brother is fifteen
and my sister is only seven. I (1) .... (✓) lots of books and some CDs. My sister
(2) .... (✓) five dolls and lots of games. My brother (3) .... (✓)
a computer but he (4) .... (✗) a personal stereo. I (5) .... (✓) a
CD player but I (6) .... (✗) a camera. My mum and dad (7) .... (✓)
a big car and a small house by the sea. We (8) .... (✓) a white cat, too.

Pairwork

Work with a partner. Tell your partner what you have or haven't got. Then tell him/her what the
members of your family have or haven't got.

Writing

Write a paragraph about yourself. Think about:
- what you have got.
- what you haven't got.

....

....

....

....

....

....

Review 1 (Units 1-4)

1

Complete the sentences with the Present Simple of **to be**.

Eg   He ....is....... very hungry. ✓

1   The light .... off now. ✓
2   The river .... near our house. ✗
3   The pens .... on the desk. ✗
4   James and Margaret .... friends. ✓

5   He .... very lucky today. ✗
6   She .... a good friend. ✓
7   I .... thirsty now. ✗
8   The trees in the garden .... very green. ✓

2

Complete the questions with **am**, **are** or **is** and write answers.

Eg   ....Is.... it cold today? ✓
      .....Yes, it is......

1   .... dinner ready? ✓
    ....

2   .... the postman at the door? ✓
    ....

3   .... we nearly home? ✗
    ....

4   .... the dogs in the garden? ✗
    ....

5   .... you at work now? ✓
    ....

6   .... the shoes under the bed? ✗
    ....

7   .... the telephone next to the bed? ✓
    ....

8   .... you happy? ✓
    ....

3

Choose the correct answer.

Eg   Is (he) / they happy?

1   They / She is English.
2   Are she / they in the car?
3   We / He aren't in the house.
4   He / I isn't in the garden.

5   I / She am a teacher.
6   Are you / he tired?
7   We / I are hungry.
8   He / I is at the gym.

4

Write sentences or questions with **to be**.

Eg   he / not be / very tired
      He isn't very tired.

1   our friends / be / at the cinema now
    ....

2   the little girl / be / ready for school / ?
    ....

3   Jim / be / very kind
    ....

4   Mrs Brown / not be / at the office now
    ....

5   you / be / sad today / ?
    ....

6   the sea / be / very cold
    ....

7   he / not be / very strong
    ....

8   the keys / be / in her bag
    ....

5

5 Put the words in the correct part of the chart.

ant   apple   bag   banana   cat   elephant   funny story   happy girl   hour
house   insect   interesting day   orange jacket   unhappy boy   wet dog   yellow chair

a	an
bag	*ant*

6 Write the plurals.

Singular	Plural
Eg *leaf*	*leaves*
1 watch	....
2 tooth	....
3 photo	....
4 sheep	....
5 man	....
6 bus	....
7 fox	....
8 brush	....
9 woman	....
10 boy	....
11 person	....
12 child	....
13 mouse	....
14 foot	....
15 party	....

7 Complete the sentences with **there is** or **there are**.

Eg   *There are* .... two pencils on the desk.

1   .... two cats in our house.
2   .... a car in the street.
3   .... a supermarket near the school.
4   .... twenty students in our class.
5   .... a nice restaurant in this street.
6   .... hundreds of apples on the tree.
7   .... five CDs in the bag.
8   .... a bird on my balcony.

Write questions and answers with **there is** or **there are**.

Eg   *a bag / on / the desk / ? ✓*
     Is there a bag on the desk?
     Yes, there is.

1   roses / in / the vase / ? ✓

     ....
     ....

2   two oranges / on / the table / ? ✗

     ....
     ....

3   a big park / opposite / your school / ? ✗

     ....
     ....

4   a black cat / under / the chair / ? ✓

     ....
     ....

5   pens / in / the drawer / ? ✗

     ....
     ....

6   a blackboard / in / the classroom / ? ✓

     ....
     ....

7   a small dog / in / his garden / ? ✓

     ....
     ....

8   nice restaurants / near / the sea / ? ✓

     ....
     ....

Find the mistakes and write the sentences correctly.

Eg   *Dad isn't in work today.*
     Dad isn't at work today.

1   There are two dogs on the middle of the road.

     ....
     ....

2   The students are not in school today.

     ....
     ....

3   There are five people in the bus stop.

     ....
     ....

4   It's the third house at the right.

     ....
     ....

5   Grandma sits on her armchair every day.

     ....
     ....

6   The picture is on the top of the page.

     ....
     ....

7   Mum is in home.

     ....
     ....

8   My sister's room is in my room and the bathroom.

     ....
     ....

22

Complete the sentences with Prepositions of Place.

Eg   *The ball is ......next to...... the chair.*

1   The ball is .... the chair.
2   The ball is .... the chair
3   The ball is .... the chair.

4   The ball is .... the two chairs.
5   The ball is .... the chair.

11

Complete the sentences with **have got**. Use the short form.

Eg   I ....'ve got......... a new bike. ✓

1   I .... a headache. ✓
2   We .... a house by the sea. ✗
3   They .... a beautiful garden. ✓
4   I .... a new dictionary. ✗
5   You .... good marks. ✓
6   She .... any brothers or sisters. ✗
7   They .... a big car. ✗
8   We .... two kittens. ✓

12

Complete the questions with **have got** and the words in brackets.

Eg   *...Have you got.... a pet? (you)*

1   .... a new car? (Mr Evans)
2   .... tickets for the cinema? (they)
3   .... a CD player? (you)
4   .... a headache? (Susan)
5   .... fair hair? (the baby)
6   .... cousins in Australia? (you)
7   .... paint on my face? (I)
8   .... a sore throat? (the boy)

Possessive Adjectives & Pronouns, 's, Demonstratives & Who's/Whose?

Possessive Adjectives

Subject Pronouns	Possessive Adjectives
I	my
you	your
he	his
she	her
it	its
we	our
you	your
they	their

We use possessive adjectives when:

- something belongs to someone.
  This is my car.

- someone has a particular relationship with someone or something.
  Gary is her brother.

Notes
We don't use *the* or *a* with possessive adjectives.
My bike is in the garden.
The bike is in the garden.

1 Complete the sentences with Possessive Adjectives.

Eg   ...*My*...... book is next to the bed. (I)

1   .... milk is in the bowl. (it)
2   .... bag is here. (you)
3   .... house is next to the café. (they)
4   .... car is blue. (we)
5   .... sister is my best friend. (he)
6   .... garden is lovely! (you)
7   .... trainers are red. (she)
8   .... bikes are big. (you)

THINK ABOUT IT!

*The Possessive Adjective **its** does not have an apostrophe. **It's** means it is.*

24

Possessive 's

We use 's to show that
something belongs to someone.
They are Ben's books.

We add 's to names or to
singular nouns.
Jill's father has got a good job.
The girl's father has got a good job.

When the noun is plural, we
add an apostrophe.
*The girls' fathers have got good
jobs.*

When the noun has an
irregular plural, we add 's.
*The children's fathers have got
good jobs.*

2 Complete the sentences with the Possessive 's ('s or ')
and the words in brackets.

Eg ....*Greg's*............ house is opposite the school. *(Greg)*

1 .... handbag is by the door. (Mary)

2 My .... name is George. (cousin)

3 His .... car is a Honda. (father)

4 The .... dog is called Bernie. (boys)

5 Their .... house is near our house. (friend)

6 The .... room is on the right. (headmaster)

7 His .... names are Bob and Joe. (brothers)

8 The .... clothes are very expensive. (men)

Possessive Pronouns

Possessive Adjectives	Possessive Pronouns
my	mine
your	yours
his	his
her	hers
its	–
our	ours
your	your
their	theirs

3 Complete the sentences with Possessive Pronouns.

Eg *The CD player is ....*mine*................ . (I)*

1 The brown case is .... (he)

2 The blue pencil is .... (you)

3 The coffee over there is .... (she)

4 The house is .... (they)

5 The money is .... (you)

6 The apples are .... (we)

We use possessive pronouns when something belongs to someone or when someone has a
particular relationship with something.
The bag is hers.

After a possessive adjective, there is always a noun. But a possessive pronoun replaces a possessive
adjective and a noun.
It's her bag. It's hers.
It's my book. The book is mine.

Demonstratives

Singular	Plural
this	these
that	those

We use demonstratives to show that something or someone is near us (*this, these*) or further away (*that, those*).
This is my bag. That bag is yours.
These pens are Sue's. Those are Helen's pens.

When we want to ask a question, we use the verb *to be*.
Is this your book? Is this book yours?
Are these Sue's pencils? Are these pencils Sue's?

4 Write sentences with **this**, **that**, **these** or **those**.

 1 apples

 2 oranges

 3 bone

 4 cake

Eg picture

 5 eggs

 6 ice cream

 7 newspaper

 8 books

Eg *That is a picture.*
....

1 ....

2 ....

3 ....

4 ....

5 ....

6 ....

7 ....

8 ....

Who's?/Whose?

We mustn't confuse *Who's ...?* and *Whose ...?*
Who's ...? means *Who is ...?*
Who's at the door? (Who is at the door?)

Whose ...? asks who something belongs to.
Whose is this key?
Whose shoes are these?

5 Choose the correct answer.

Eg Who's /(Whose) bag is this?

1 *Who's / Whose pens are these?*

2 *Who's / Whose on the phone?*

3 *Who's / Whose at the door?*

4 *Who's / Whose are those books?*

5 *Who's / Whose ticket is this?*

6 *Who's / Whose at home?*

6 Rewrite the sentences.

Eg *These are my pens.* ....*They're mine.*...............
    This is her calculator. ....*It's hers.*...............

1 Those are his trousers. ....

2 This is her car. ....

3 That is their dog. ....

4 Those are our sandwiches. ....

5 That is my English book. ....

6 These are your CDs. ....

7 This is our new house. ....

8 Those are your clothes. ....

9 Those are my trainers. ....

10 Those are their games. ....

THINK ABOUT IT!

We can say:
Whose is this cat? *or*
Whose cat is this?

7 Choose the correct answer.

Eg ..... *is this pencil?*
    a Who's   **b** Whose   **c** Who

1 Is this your car?
   Yes, it's ..... .
   a our   **b** we   **c** ours

2 This book is ..... .
   a Jim's   **b** the Jim's   **c** Jim

3 ..... apples are green.
   a That   **b** Mine   **c** Those

4 The CDs are ..... .
   a they   **b** theirs   **c** their

5 ..... parents have got a shop.
   a Hers   **b** Her   **c** Whose

6 ..... Jill's clothes?
   a Are these **b** These are **c** Is this

Pairwork

Work with a partner. Find five objects in your bag or pockets and put them on the table in front of you. Talk about the objects. For example:
This is my pen. It's mine.
This is your book. It's yours.

Take turns to talk about all the objects. Ask your teacher if you don't know the word for an object.

Writing

Write ten sentences or questions about yourself, your family and friends using the language you have learnt in this unit.

1 ....   6 ....

2 ....   7 ....

3 ....   8 ....

4 ....   9 ....

5 ....   10 ....

27

Present Simple

Affirmative	Negative	Question
I want	I do not (don't) want	Do I want?
you want	you do not (don't) want	Do you want?
he wants	he does not (doesn't) want	Does he want?
she wants	she does not (doesn't) want	Does she want?
it wants	it does not (doesn't) want	Does it want?
we want	we do not (don't) want	Do we want?
you want	you do not (don't) want	Do you want?
they want	they do not (don't) want	Do they want?

Short answers

Yes, I do.	No, I don't.
Yes, you do.	No, you don't.
Yes, he does.	No, he doesn't.
Yes, she does.	No, she doesn't.
Yes, it does.	No, it doesn't.
Yes, we do.	No, we don't.
Yes, you do.	No, you don't.
Yes, they do.	No, they don't.

We use the Present Simple to talk about:

■ permanent states.
My mother lives in Birmingham.

■ things we do often.
He visits his grandparents every weekend.

■ general truths.
It gets hot in Spain in the summer.

In the third person singular affirmative *(he, she, it)*, we add -s to the verb.

find → *finds*
laugh → *laughs*

We add -es to verbs which end in -ss, -sh, -ch, -x and -o in the third person singular affirmative.

press → *presses*
wash → *washes*
watch → *watches*
fix → *fixes*
do → *does*

When a verb ends in a consonant + -y, we take off the -y and add -ies in the third person singular affirmative.

tidy → *tidies*
marry → *marries*

When a verb ends in a vowel + -y, we just add -s in the third person singular affirmative.

say → *says*

In the negative and question forms, we use the auxiliary verb *do/does* and the main verb in its infinitive form.
They don't swim in the winter.
David doesn't like spaghetti.
Do you work on Saturdays?
Does Helen go to school on Sundays?

In short answers, we only use *do/does*. We don't use the main verb.
Do you like the theatre? Yes, I do.
Does he eat fish? No, he doesn't.

1 Complete the chart.

Verb	3rd Person Singular
play	*plays*
wash	
miss	
live	
fix	
fly	
know	
write	
do	
watch	
buy	

2 Complete the sentences with the negative form of the Present Simple.

Eg I ...... *I don't like* ...... chicken. (like).

1 They .... football. (play)
2 He .... history. (teach)
3 We .... a lot of television. (watch)
4 She .... to the gym. (go)
5 You .... a lot of fruit. (eat)
6 I .... French. (speak)
7 She .... a bike to work. (ride)
8 He .... cola. (drink)

3 Complete the questions with the Present Simple and write answers.

Eg ...... *Do you like* ...... pop music? (you / like) ✔
...... *Yes, I do* ....

1 .... the words? (he / know) ✔
....
2 .... meat? (they / eat) ✗
....
3 .... nice? (I / look) ✔
....
4 .... tennis? (she / play) ✗
....

5 .... letters to them? (you / write) ✔
....
6 .... a lot of clothes? (they / buy) ✗
....
7 .... a big car? (that woman / drive) ✔
....
8 .... well? (your father / cook) ✗
....

Adverbs of Frequency

When we talk about habits or we want to say how often something happens, we use adverbs of frequency. The adverbs of frequency are:

never	sometimes	often	usually	always
0% ←				→ 100%

Adverbs of frequency usually come before the main verb, unless the verb is *to be*.
I often go to the cinema.
He is usually late for work.

Time expressions such as *every day, every week, once a week, on Mondays,* etc usually go at the beginning or the end of a sentence.
He walks to work every day.
On Mondays she plays basketball.

4 Write the words in the correct order.

Eg   *she / basketball / plays / often*
    She often plays basketball.
....

1   late / they / for dinner / never / are
....

2   Tom / wears / usually / jeans
....

3   take us / our parents / sometimes / to school / by car
....

4   wear / that silly hat / you / do / always / ?
....

5   Fiona / for tea / often / cakes / makes
....

6   usually / I / not / have / at this time / breakfast / do
....

7   busy / the doctor / always / is / ?
....

8   not / our parents / go swimming / do / often
....

Prepositions of Time

at	on	in
at six o'clock	on Saturdays	in the morning
at night	on Monday mornings	in the afternoon
at the weekend	on 5th May	in the evening
at Christmas	on my birthday	in 1987
at Easter	on Christmas Day	in the winter
		in June
		in the holidays

5 Complete the sentences with **at, on** or **in**.

Eg *He goes to the beach every day ......in........ the holidays.*

1   .... Christmas we visit our friends in London.

2   He plays football .... Sundays.

3   I have an English lesson .... seven o'clock .... the evening.

4   We go on holiday .... the winter.

5   They often go to the cinema .... the weekend.

6   My birthday is .... 13th February.

7   She swims .... the summer.

8   He wakes up early .... Saturday mornings and goes shopping.

9   Do you go to bed late .... night?

10   I always have a party .... my birthday.

6 Write sentences with the Present Simple.

Eg   Jim / wash / the car / Saturdays
     Jim washes the car on Saturdays.
     ....

1   Jim and Tonic / not go / to work / Sundays
     ....
     ....

2   Tonic / never / eat / fish
     ....
     ....

3   Jim / always / help / people / ?
     ....
     ....

4   Jim and Tonic / play / football / the weekend
     ....
     ....

5   Jim / sometimes / watch TV / the evenings
     ....
     ....

6   Jim and Tonic / often / clean / the house / Fridays
     ....
     ....

7 Complete the sentences with one word in each gap.

Eg   *Jim does not wake up at the same time ......every...... day.*

1   I .... not like strawberry ice cream.

2   The children have English lessons .... Mondays and Wednesdays.

3   We have cereal and milk for breakfast .... day.

4   .... your best friend live near you?

5   They do .... usually go out on Sunday evenings.

6   The sun is very hot .... the summer.

7   Peter .... not work in a bank.

8   Do you watch TV late .... night?

8 Write the words in the correct order.

Eg *often / chess / she / with a friend / plays*
She often plays chess with a friend.
....

1 on holiday / go / they / never / January / in
....

2 Saturdays / goes / usually / she / on / out / with her friends
....

3 they / spaghetti / eat / do / often / ?
....

4 have / doesn't / the / at / she / English lessons / weekend
....

5 sometimes / see / I / my aunt / after school
....

6 see / he / every / doesn't / his best friend / week
....

9 Find the mistakes and write the sentences correctly.

Eg *He like basketball.*
He likes basketball.
....

1 You want an ice cream?
....

2 They not go on holiday every year.
....

3 Do he often goes to the gym?
....

4 He is catches the train every day.
....

5 They finish school on June.
....

6 She don't want pizza today.
....

10 Complete the text with the Present Simple.

My big brother is funny. He (Eg) ....*likes*............ (like) football but he
(1) .... (not like) basketball. He (2) .... (not study) a lot
but he (3) .... (get) good marks at university. He (4) ....
(not tidy) his room but he (5) .... (tidy) his desk. He
(6) .... (talk) a lot but he often (7) .... (want) to be quiet
and read a book. I (8) .... (not understand) my brother!

32

11 Complete the sentences with the Present Simple.

Eg   I ....*don't like*........ vegetables. *(not like)*

1   .... you .... every day? *(study)*

2   He often .... football on television. *(watch)*

3   They .... to the gym on Sundays. *(not go)*

4   .... she .... a lot of books? *(read)*

5   He usually .... a lot of fish when he goes fishing. *(catch)*

6   .... they .... their friends often? *(visit)*

7   I .... football. I play volleyball. *(not play)*

8   She .... sweets, but she likes cakes. *(not like)*

Pairwork

Work with a partner. Take turns to ask and answer the following questions:

- Do you live in a flat or a house?
- Have you got any brothers or sisters?
- What do you do in the mornings?
- What do you do in the evenings?
- What do you do in your free time?

- Do you like music?
- Do you play the piano?
- Do you like sport?
- Do you play football?
- Do you read lots of books?

Writing

Write a paragraph about your partner using his/her answers from the
questions above.

....

....

....

....

....

....

....

....

Adverbs, Too & Enough

This is my philosophy, Tonic. Work hard and play hard. Sleep well. Sing loudly. Eat healthily. And drive carefully!

I agree, Jim.

Adverbs

Adjectives	Adverbs
bad	badly
soft	softly
careful	carefully
nice	nicely
noisy	noisily
simple	simply
hard	hard
fast	fast
late	late
early	early
good	well

Adverbs describe how we do something.
She drives her car carefully.

We usually make adverbs by adding *-ly* to the adjective.

quick	➔	*quickly*
helpful	➔	*helpfully*

When the adjective ends in *-y*, we take off the *-y* and add *-ily*.

easy	➔	*easily*

When the adjective ends in *-le*, we take off the *-e* and add *-y*.

simple	➔	*simply*

Some adverbs don't end in *-ly* and have the same form as the adjective.

hard	➔	*hard*	*fast*	➔	*fast*
early	➔	*early*	*late*	➔	*late*

Some adverbs don't end in *-ly* and have a different form from the adjective.

good	➔	*well*

Adverbs that describe how we do something usually go after the main verb.
He runs quickly around the park every morning.

1 Complete the chart.

Adjectives	Adverbs
quick	quickly
heavy	
slow	
terrible	
angry	
polite	
useful	
light	
quiet	
happy	
sad	
hard	
good	

2 Complete the sentences with Adverbs.

Eg He talks very ....quickly............ when he's on the phone. (quick)

1 Please play ...., children. I've got a headache. (quiet)
2 She does very .... in her exams. (good)
3 Drive .... on your way home! (careful)
4 The teacher explains .... (slow)
5 I run .... (fast)
6 I usually get up .... on Sundays. (late)
7 Those children speak .... (polite)
8 The little boy plays .... with his toys every day. (happy)
9 Jim sings .... in the bath. (loud)
10 She plays the piano .... (bad)

Too and Enough

Too has a negative meaning. It means very much, more than is necessary or wanted.
I can't lift that box. It's too heavy.

We usually use the word too to say that someone is too small, big, slow, etc to do something. We use:

too + adjective/adverb + to + verb.
She's too young to go to a nightclub.

Enough has a positive meaning. It means as many/much as is necessary or wanted. It goes before a noun but after an adjective or adverb.
There are enough chairs in the room.
She can pass her exam. She's clever enough.
He can win the race. He's fast enough.

We often use the word enough to say that someone or something is small, big, slow, etc enough to do something. We use:

adjective/adverb + enough + to + verb
It's warm enough to go swimming today.

enough + noun + to + verb.
I've got enough money to buy a new CD.

3 Complete the sentences with **too** and the words in brackets.

Eg   He's .... *too lazy to study* .... hard. (lazy, study)

1   I'm .... for lunch. (hungry, wait)
2   It's .... a picnic. (cold, have)
3   They're .... 'no'. (polite, say)
4   The exercise is .... (difficult, do)
5   The coat is .... (expensive, buy)
6   The food is .... (hot, eat)
7   I'm .... this dress! (young, wear)
8   She's .... out. (tired, go)

4 Complete the sentences with **enough** and the words in brackets.

Eg   *The weather isn't* .... *warm enough to go* .... *out. (warm, go)*

1   He isn't .... all his exams. (clever, pass)
2   It isn't .... swimming. (hot, go)
3   She isn't .... the race. (fast, win)
4   The painting is .... on the wall. (good, put)
5   The little girl isn't .... the door. (tall, open)
6   The boy is .... a car. (old, drive)

5 Complete the sentences with **enough** and the words in brackets.

Eg   *There isn't* .... *enough food to feed* .... *thirty children. (food, feed)*

1   Have you got .... those trainers? (money, buy)
2   I haven't got .... the bicycle now. (time, mend)
3   We've got .... to all the children. (sweets, give)
4   Have they got .... the party this weekend? (time, have)
5   Tonic has got .... with. (bones, play)

6 Choose the correct answer.

Eg   *There aren't ..... for everyone.*
      a sandwiches enough   ⓑ enough sandwiches

1   My mother is ..... to come to the meeting.
     a too busy   **b** busy enough
2   The boys work very ..... .
     a slow   **b** slowly
3   She speaks English very ..... .
     a badly   **b** good

4   The beds are ..... .
     a softly   **b** soft enough
5   The book is too difficult ..... .
     a to read   **b** read
6   He plays football ..... .
     a well   **b** good

Match and write sentences.

Eg *He is not old enough to*   a   beautifully.
1   The children shout   b   to go for a walk.
2   It's raining too hard   c   fast along this road.
3   There isn't enough   d   every Saturday.
4   People drive   e   loudly at break time.
5   She sings   f   orange juice for all our friends.
6   He plays basketball   g   *drive a car.*

THINK ABOUT IT!

He works very hard means that someone works a lot.
He works too hard means that someone works more than they should.

Eg *He is not old enough to drive a car.* ....

1   ....

2   ....

3   ....

4   ....

5   ....

6   ....

Pairwork

Work with a partner. Take turns to ask and answer the following questions:

- Do you get up early or late on work/school days?
- Do you go to bed early or late on work/school days?
- Do you get up early or late at the weekend?
- Do you go to bed early or late at the weekend?
- Do you play football well or badly?

- Do you sing beautifully?
- Do you drive your car/ride your bike carefully or carelessly?
- Do you speak English well or badly?

Writing

Write a paragraph about yourself using your answers from the questions above.

....

....

....

....

....

....

37

Present Continuous

Present Continuous

Affirmative	Negative	Question
I am (I'm) eating	I am not (I'm not) eating	Am I eating?
you are (you're) eating	you are not (aren't) eating	Are you eating?
he is (he's) eating	he is not (isn't) eating	Is he eating?
she is (she's) eating	she is not (isn't) eating	Is she eating?
it is (it's) eating	it is not (isn't) eating	Is it eating?
we are (we're) eating	we are not (aren't) eating	Are we eating?
you are (you're) eating	you are not (aren't) eating	Are you eating?
they are (they're) eating	they are not (aren't) eating	Are they eating?

Short answers

Yes, I am.	No, I'm not.
Yes, you are.	No, you aren't.
Yes, he is.	No, he isn't.
Yes, she is.	No, she isn't.
Yes, it isn't.	No, it isn't.
Yes, we are.	No, we aren't.
Yes, you are.	No, you aren't.
Yes, they are.	No, they aren't.

We use the Present Continuous to talk about:

- things that are in progress at the time of speaking.
  What are they doing? They're eating their lunch.

- things that are in progress around the time of speaking or that are temporary.
  He's looking for a new flat.

The Present Continuous is formed with *am/are/is* and the main verb with the *-ing* ending.

jump → jumping

When the main verb ends in -e, we take off the -e and add *-ing*.

make → making

When the verb ends in a consonant and before that consonant there is a vowel, we double the final consonant and add *-ing*.

win → winning

When the verb ends in *-l*, we double the *-l* and add *-ing*.

cancel → cancelling

When the verb ends in *-ie*, we take off the *-ie* and add *-y* and *-ing*.

tie → tying
lie → lying
die → dying

Notes

We can use time expressions such as *now, at the moment, these days, at present, today,* etc with the Present Continuous.

She's washing her car at the moment.

---

1 Make the **-ing** form of the verbs and put them in the correct part of the chart.

carry   close   come   draw   drive   get   give   go
leave   open   play   put   ride
run   sit   stop   study   swim

hit hitting	write writing	work working
getting	closing	carrying

2
Complete the sentences with the Present Continuous.

Eg   I *am talking* .... to my friend at the moment. (talk)

1   They .... letters to their friends. (write)

2   Mum .... lunch ready. (get)

3   The boys .... their bikes in the street. (ride)

4   I .... a picture of the flowers. (draw)

5   Where's Dad? He .... on the balcony. (sit)

6   The children .... hard for the test. (study)

7   She .... how to use a computer. (learn)

8   We .... in France at present. (live)

3
Complete the sentences with the negative form of the Present Continuous.

Eg   Jim *isn't playing* .... football at the moment. (play)

1   They .... to the cassette. (listen)

2   She .... very hard. (work)

3   We .... fish for lunch. (have)

4   It .... today. (snow)

5   I .... breakfast now. (make)

6   The babies .... at the moment. (sleep)

7   He .... his mother to clean the house today. (help)

8   You .... any work. Come and help me! (do)

4
Complete the questions with the Present Continuous and write answers.

Eg   .... *Is mum cooking* .... lunch? (mum / cook) ✓
    ....

1   .... at you? (the baby / smile) ✓
    ....

2   .... a good time? (you / have) ✓
    ....

3   .... the exercise in their books? (the students / do) ✗
    ....

4   .... at the moment? (he / eat) ✗
    ....

5   .... for the bus? (they / wait) ✓
    ....

6   .... outside? (it / rain) ✗
    ....

7   .... now? (you / leave) ✗
    ....

8   .... on your computer? (your sister / play) ✓
    ....

5 Write sentences with the Present Continuous.

Eg

2

4

6

1

3

5

7

8

Eg   *Jim / read / the newspaper*
Jim is reading the newspaper.

1   Tonic / eat / his bone
....
....

2   Dad / wash / the car
....
....

3   the cat / drink / coffee
....
....

4   it / rain / outside
....
....

5   the children / play / tennis
....
....

6   he / run / at the gym
....
....

7   Jim / drive / his car
....
....

8   the children / swim / in the pool
....
....

Pairwork

Work with a partner. It is eight o'clock on a Saturday evening. Your partner, your partner's family and a few friends are at his/her house. Ask your partner what everyone is doing.

Writing

Write a short e-mail to a friend. Tell him/her:

- what you are doing at the moment.
- what the weather is like.
- what the members of your family are doing.

41

Review 2 (Units 5-8)

1 Complete the chart.

Subject Pronouns	Possessive Adjectives	Possessive Pronouns
I	*my*	*mine*
you		
he		
she		
it		
we		
you		
they		

2 Complete the sentences with Possessive Adjectives.

Eg   ....*My*....... *pen is on the table. (I)*

1   .... brother is my best friend. (she)
2   .... new coat is very nice. (you)
3   .... trainers are black. (he)
4   .... tail is long. (it)
5   .... coffee is over there. (she)
6   .... camera is new. (I)
7   .... house is next to the school. (they)
8   .... car is silver. (we)

3 Complete the sentences with Possessive Pronouns.

Eg   *It's my cassette. It's* ....*mine*............ .

1   They're your cakes. They're ....
2   They're our sweets. They're ....
3   They're his trousers. They're ....
4   It's her bag. It's ....
5   It's his computer. It's ....
6   They're my biscuits. They're ....
7   It's her cup of tea. It's ....
8   It's their flat. It's ....

4 Complete the sentences with the Present Simple.

Eg   I ....*come*.............. from Dublin. *(come)*

1   You .... a lot of bread. *(eat)*

2   Jim .... Spanish. *(not speak)*

3   My parents .... to work by bus. *(not go)*

4   Helen .... coffee every morning. *(drink)*

5   My friends .... chess. *(not play)*

6   She .... geography. *(teach)*

7   Susan and I .... a lot of clothes every year. *(buy)*

8   We .... in Birmingham. *(not live)*

5 Complete the questions with the Present Simple and write answers.

Eg   *Do you like* .... *classical music? (you / like)* ✓
     Yes, I do. ....

1   .... to your grandparents every month? *(you / write)* ✓
    ....

2   .... a lot of people? *(they / know)* ✗
    ....

3   .... her car? *(Sheila / often / wash)* ✓
    ....

4   .... nice meals? *(Danny / always/ cook)* ✓
    ....

5   .... to music? *(he / often / listen)* ✗
    ....

6   .... a lot of fruit? *(the parrot / eat)* ✓
    ....

7   .... an ice cream? *(you / want)* ✗
    ....

8   .... a car? *(she / drive)* ✓
    ....

6 Choose the correct answer.

Eg   *What time do you get up* in */ at the mornings?*

1   *In / At* winter, we go skiing.

2   They often go out for a meal *on / at* the weekend.

3   His birthday is *at / in* September.

4   She goes to the beach *on / in* the summer.

5   We open our presents early *on / at* Christmas Day.

6   He goes to the gym *at / on* Saturdays.

7   I usually have a maths lesson *to / at* eight o'clock.

8   He travels a lot *at / in* the holidays.

Complete the sentences with **too** and the words in brackets.

Eg   I am ....*too tired to go*............ out with you. (tired, go)

1   The jacket is ....
    (old, wear)

2   The spaghetti is ....
    (hot, eat)

3   The books are ....
    (heavy, carry)

4   She's .... her friends.
    (busy, visit)

5   It's .... out. (wet, go)

6   He's .... (young, understand)

7   The song is ....
    (difficult, learn)

8   It's .... a picnic.
    (cold, have)

Complete the chart.

Adjectives	Adverbs
quick	*quickly*
heavy	
slow	
simple	
horrible	
angry	
polite	
beautiful	
light	
quiet	
happy	
easy	
late	
good	
hard	
fast	

Rewrite the sentences using the word given.

Eg   The exercise is too difficult to do. **easy**
     The exercise ....*is not easy enough*............ to do.

1   The soup is too hot to drink. **cool**
    The soup ....
    to drink.

2   The students are not old enough to understand
    the lesson. **young**
    The students ....
    the lesson.

3   The children are too short to reach the top
    shelf. **tall**
    The children ....
    to reach the top shelf.

4   The bed is too hard for me. **soft**
    The bed ....
    for me.

5   The bag is too heavy to lift easily. **light**
    The bag ....
    to lift easily.

6   The girl is too slow to win the race. **fast**
    The girl ....
    to win the race.

10 Complete the sentences with **enough** and the words in brackets.

Eg   There aren't *enough good programmes to watch* on television. (good programmes, watch)

1   Jim has got .... (books, read)

2   Have you got .... that necklace? (money, buy)

3   I haven't got .... your homework now. (time, check)

4   We've got .... to all the children. (cakes, give)

5   There isn't .... in the sandwiches. (ham, put)

6   Has she got .... a cake? (eggs, make)

11 Complete the sentences with the Present Continuous.

Eg   The sun ....*is shining*............ brightly today. (shine)

1   They .... letters to their cousins in America. (write)

2   .... Mum .... breakfast ready? (get)

3   They .... to music. (not listen)

4   The girl .... the dog for a walk. (take)

5   We .... soup for lunch. (not have)

6   It .... today. (not rain)

7   I .... that mountain over there. (paint)

8   She .... late tonight. (not work)

12 Complete the questions with the Present Continuous and write answers.

Eg   ....*Is Mum ironing*........ the clothes? (Mum / iron) ✓
    ....*Yes, she is.*........ .

1   .... for the bus? (the people / run) ✓
    ....

2   .... outside? (it / snow) ✗
    ....

3   .... at the moment? (you / study) ✓
    ....

4   .... on the computer? (your friend / play) ✗
    ....

5   .... ? (the baby / sleep) ✗
    ....

6   .... a party? (you / have) ✗
    ....

7   .... the students' compositions? (Miss Harris / mark) ✓
    ....

8   .... their homework? (they / do) ✗
    ....

45

Present Simple & Present Continuous

I do the same things every day. I go for a walk, I dig for my bone, I have my dinner and I go to sleep.

But today, I'm flying a helicopter and Jim is teaching me! I love surprises!

Present Simple and Present Continuous

	Affirmative	**Negative**	**Question**
Present Simple	I eat he eats	I do not (don't) eat he does not (doesn't) eat	Do I eat? Does he eat?
Present Continuous	I am (I'm) eating he is (he's) eating	I am not (I'm not) eating he is not (he isn't) eating	Am I eating? Is he eating?

We use the Present Simple to talk about:

■ permanent situations.
My brother works in London.

■ habits.
I go to the gym every day.

■ general truths.
Lions eat meat.

We use the Present Continuous to talk about:

■ things that are in progress at the time we are speaking.
She's making lunch now.

■ things that are in progress around the time of speaking or that are temporary.
They're painting the garage at the moment.

Time Expressions

We often use adverbs of frequency (*never, sometimes, often, usually, always*) and time expressions such as *at the weekend, on Saturdays, every day, in the mornings, in the summer,* etc with the Present Simple.
He usually leaves for work at eight o'clock.
They go for long walks at the weekend.

We often use time expressions such as *now, at the moment, these days, at present, this term, this year, tonight,* etc with the Present Continuous.
I am watching the news at the moment.
He's working very hard this term.

1 Complete the sentences with the Present Simple.

Eg He *doesn't want* his breakfast. (not want)

1   They .... very hot weather. (not like)

2   .... you .... that boy over there? (know)

3   She .... very fast. (run)

4   .... he .... in England? (live)

5   They .... French lessons on Fridays. (not have)

6   She .... coffee. (not like)

7   .... you .... Spanish? (speak)

8   They .... by train. (always travel)

2 Complete the sentences with the Present Continuous.

Eg They *are building* a house near the sea. (build)

1   .... they .... French or German? (learn)

2   She .... supper this evening. (not cook)

3   The children .... pictures of fruit and vegetables. (draw)

4   I .... the news on television. (watch)

5   He .... a new computer game at the moment. (play)

6   Where is Susan? .... she .... her friends? (visit)

7   The students .... hard this term. (not work)

8   I .... a letter. (not write)

3 Put the words and expressions in the correct part of the chart.

always   at present   at the moment   every day   in the winter   now
    often   on Sundays   this month   this term   this year   usually

Present Simple	Present Continuous
always	*now*

47

Write sentences with the Present Simple and Present Continuous.

Eg *Jim / usually / get up / seven o'clock / but today he / sleep*

Jim usually gets up at seven o'clock
but today he is sleeping.
....
....

1 Jim / usually / go to the gym / eight o'clock / but today he / have breakfast

....
....
....
....

2 Jim / usually / leave for work / nine o'clock / but this morning he / water the flowers / in his garden

....
....
....
....

3 Jim / usually / take Tonic for a walk / the evenings / but this evening he / play with Tonic / in the park

....
....
....
....

4 Jim / usually / read a book / in bed / but tonight he / dance with his friends

....
....
....
....

5 Complete the sentences with the Present Simple or Present Continuous.

Eg It's nine o'clock and they ............ the shop now. (open)

1 He never .... on Saturdays. (work)
2 .... the sun .... at the moment? (shine)
3 He .... the heavy bags. (always / not carry)
4 She's got a headache and she .... down. (lie)
5 I .... my friends at the weekend. (often / visit)
6 She .... her new job today. (not begin)
7 We .... presents to our family at Christmas. (give)
8 .... he .... to go on the school trip? (want)

THINK
ABOUT IT!

*Don't forget the spelling rule:
If a verb ends with one vowel
and one consonant, then we
double the consonant before
we add -ing.*

6 Choose the correct answer.

Eg *I wake up at the same time* at the moment / (every day.)

1 Look! She *runs / is running* to catch the bus.
2 We are not working *at the moment / in the mornings*. We are on holiday.
3 *Do you play / Are you playing* with your friend every day?
4 They are visiting their aunt *at the moment / on Saturdays*.
5 Every morning she *goes / is going* for a run around the park.
6 Do you go to work by bus *today / every day*?
7 It's cold this morning and we *wear / are wearing* our coats.
8 I don't come here *often / this afternoon*.

Pairwork

Work with a partner. Ask your partner what he/she usually does
at the weekend.

Writing

Write a paragraph about yourself. Think about:

■ what you usually do at the weekend.
■ what you are doing now.

....
....
....
....
....
....
....

Can & Must

Can for Ability & Permission

Affirmative	Negative	Question
I can swim	I cannot (can't) swim	Can I swim?
you can swim	you cannot (can't) swim	Can you swim?
he can swim	he cannot (can't) swim	Can he swim?
she can swim	she cannot (can't) swim	Can she swim?
it can swim	it cannot (can't) swim	Can it swim?
we can swim	we cannot (can't) swim	Can we swim?
you can swim	you cannot (can't) swim	Can you swim?
they can swim	they cannot (can't) swim	Can they swim?

Short answers

Yes, I can.	No, I can't.
Yes, you can.	No, you can't.
Yes, he can.	No, he can't.
Yes, she can.	No, she can't.
Yes, it can.	No, it can't.
Yes, we can.	No, we can't.
Yes, you can.	No, you can't.
Yes, they can.	No, they can't.

We use *can* and *can't* to talk about ability.
They are followed by a bare infinitive.
I can sing.
You can play the piano.
Can he draw?

We also use *can* to ask for or give permission
to do something.
Can I stay at my friend's house at the weekend?
You can borrow my car.

We use *can* to talk about the present and the
future.
I can go to the shops now.
She can come to our party next week.

Notes
We often use *can* with verbs of feeling, such as
see, hear, smell, etc.
Can you see the bus?
I can hear the phone ringing.

1 Complete the sentences with **can** and the verbs in brackets.

Eg   I ....can........ run 100 metres. (run)

1   .... you .... French? (speak)
2   They .... to the concert on Friday. (not come)
3   He .... me with the bags. (help)
4   She .... her keys. (not find)
5   .... they .... well? (swim)
6   I .... the guitar. (not play)
7   We .... on holiday this year. (not go)
8   .... you .... the sea from the village? (see)

2 Complete the sentences with **can** and the verbs in brackets.

Eg   ...Can... she ...buy... some chocolates after school? (buy)

1   You .... to music now. It's late! (not listen)
2   It's hot! .... I .... the window? (open)
3   You .... a new watch for your birthday. (have)
4   .... we .... our friends to the house on Saturday? (invite)
5   .... I .... the match this evening? (watch)
6   You .... out now. Do your homework! (not go)
7   .... they .... a new pair of jeans on Saturday? (buy)
8   You .... up late tonight. You have school tomorrow. (not stay)

3 Write questions and answers.

Eg   you / cook a meal? ✓
   ..Can you cook a meal..........?
   ..Yes, I can..........

1   they / swim? ✓
   ....?
   ....

2   he / play the violin? ✗
   ....?
   ....

3   she / speak Italian? ✓
   ....?
   ....

4   you / ride a horse? ✓
   ....?
   ....

5   we / have a pizza? ✓
   ....?
   ....

6   I / close the window? ✓
   ....?
   ....

7   they / watch TV? ✗
   ....?
   ....

8   she / come with us? ✓
   ....?
   ....

51

Must for Obligation & Prohibition

Affirmative	Negative	Question
I must go	I must not (mustn't) go	Must I go?
you must go	you must not (mustn't) go	Must you go?
he must go	he must not (mustn't) go	Must he go?
she must go	she must not (mustn't) go	Must she go?
it must go	it must not (mustn't) go	Must it go?
we must go	we must not (mustn't) go	Must we go?
you must go	you must not (mustn't) go	Must you go?
they must go	they must not (mustn't) go	Must they go?

Short answers

Yes, I must.	No, I mustn't.
Yes, you must.	No, you mustn't.
Yes, he must.	No, he mustn't.
Yes, she must.	No, she mustn't.
Yes, it must.	No, it mustn't.
Yes, we must.	No, we mustn't.
Yes, you must.	No, you mustn't.
Yes, they must.	No, they mustn't.

We use *must* to talk about obligation. *Must* is followed by a bare infinitive.
I must go to the dentist.
She must visit her parents this weekend.

We use *mustn't* to talk about things we are not allowed to do (prohibition). *Mustn't* is also followed by a bare infinitive.
I mustn't be late.
You mustn't drive too fast.

We use *must* to talk about the present and the future.
You must stop writing now.
We must go to the bank tomorrow.

Notes
It is not very polite to use *must* when we are talking to someone we don't know well or to someone who is older than us.

---

4 Complete the sentences with **must** or **mustn't**.

Eg   You *mustn't* smoke in this building. ✗

1   You .... take photos in the museum. ✗

2   You .... cross the street at the zebra crossing. ✓

3   You .... park here. ✗

4   You .... wear a helmet on a motorbike. ✓

5   You .... talk in the library. ✗

6   You .... put your litter in the bin. ✓

7   You .... take your dog with you to a restaurant. ✗

8   You .... look after your pet. ✓

5 Write sentences with **must**.

Eg *we / go to school / every day* ✓
We must go to school every day.

1 you / talk in class ✗
....

2 I / do my homework / now ✓
....

3 we / go home / soon ✓
....

4 you / finish your work / this evening?
....

5 they / make a lot of noise ✗
....

6 she / forget her books ✗
....

7 I / eat all this meat?
....

8 he / help his father in the shop?
....

9 I / be late for school ✗
....

10 we / stick pictures on the walls ✗
....

THINK ABOUT IT!

*We never put **to** after **must**.*

6 Write questions with **must** or **can**.

Eg *Must they listen to their teachers?*
Yes, they must listen to their teachers.

1 ....
No, they can't snowboard.

2 ....
Yes, they must wear school uniform.

3 ....
Yes, they can join the drama club.

4 ....
Yes, he must be on time for work.

5 ....
No, they can't use mobile phones in class.

Writing

Write a short article about your friends. Think about:

- what they *can / can't* do.
- what they *must / mustn't* do.

....
....
....
....
....
....
....
....

Pairwork

Work with a partner.
Using *can*, take turns to ask
and answer about these things:

- play the piano
- use a computer well
- understand English films
- fix a car
- use an English dictionary

Imperative, Let's & Object Pronouns

Imperative

We use the imperative when:

■ we give instructions.
Write your name here.
Take your umbrella with you; it's raining outside!

■ we want to prevent something bad from happening.
Don't touch that: it's very hot!

We form the imperative with the bare infinitive. It is the same for when we are talking to one person as it is when we are talking to many people.
Stand up, everyone!
Turn on the light, George!
Close the door!

We form the negative imperative with the word *don't*.
Don't run!
Don't talk in the library!

We often use the word *please* to be more polite.
Please hold my bag.
Please sit down.

Complete the sentences with the Imperative of the words in the box.

ask   be   close   do   eat   go   look   make   open   sit

Eg   ....*Open*......... your books at page 20. ✓
Eg   ....*Don't be*......... rude. ✗

1   .... the window, please. ✓
2   Please .... a noise. ✗
3   .... a lot of chocolates. ✗
4   .... the teacher if you don't understand. ✓

5   .... all the exercises now. ✗
6   .... to your room at once! ✓
7   .... at this photo! Isn't it funny? ✓
8   .... near the fire. It's hot! ✗

Complete the sentences with **Let's** or **Let's not** and the words in the box.

be   buy   cook   go (x2)
have   phone   watch

Eg   ....*Let's phone*......... our friends! ✓
      ....*Let's not buy*......... a CD for his birthday again! ✗

1   .... the film on TV tonight. ✓
2   .... for a walk. It's raining. ✗
3   .... a party! ✓
4   .... late for the concert! ✗
5   .... a meal for our friends! ✓
6   .... out today. ✗

Let's

We use *Let's* with the bare infinitive when we want to suggest something.
Let's go to the theatre!
Let's have an ice cream!

We form the negative with the word *not*.
It goes after *Let's* and before the infinitive.
Let's not go out tonight.
Let's not walk. Let's drive.

Object Pronouns

Subject Pronouns	Object Pronouns
I	me
you	you
he	him
she	her
it	it
we	us
you	you
they	them

We use object pronouns to replace an object in a sentence.
He is opening the book. He is opening it.
I see my friend every Saturday. I see him every Saturday.

Complete the sentences with Object Pronouns.

Eg   I like ....*them*......... very much. (Jim and Tonic)
1   She helps .... with my homework. (I)
2   I can't see .... (the boat)
3   Can you read .... in a week? (five books)
4   I can't hear .... in the kitchen. (my mother)
5   She likes .... (Tim)
6   Have you got .... in your bag? (the CDs)
7   They can't see .... from over there. (we)
8   They don't want .... (the cake)

Find the mistakes and write the sentences correctly.

Eg *Let's going to the cinema.*
   Let's go to the cinema.
   ....

1 Let's eat not now. Let's eat later.
   ....

2 I saw he at the supermarket.
   ....

3 Don't you open the window, please.
   ....

4 Sit down and you open your books.
   ....

5 Tonic likes they very much.
   ....

6 Let's to have a picnic tomorrow!
   ....

5 Rewrite the sentences using the Imperative.

Eg *You must sit down.*
   Sit down.
   ....

1 You mustn't eat all those sweets.
   ....

2 You must finish your homework.
   ....

3 You mustn't eat a lot of fast food.
   ....

4 You must cut the paper into three pieces.
   ....

5 You mustn't listen to her!
   ....

6 Complete the sentences with **Let's** or **Let's not** and the words in the box.

clean   listen   look
  phone   play   watch

Eg

1
2   3

4   5

Eg ....*Let's look*........ at the flowers in the garden. ✓

1 .... the house now. ✗
2 .... tennis! ✓
3 .... TV this evening. ✗
4 .... to some music. ✓
5 .... our friends! ✓

7 Rewrite the sentences using Object Pronouns.

THINK ABOUT IT!

*We can put the word **please** at the beginning or at the end of a sentence.*

Eg   *Don't eat those eggs!*
      Don't eat them! ....

1   Please have <u>this piece of cake</u>.
      ....

2   Let's phone <u>Jill</u> now!
      ....

3   Can you see <u>George</u>?
      ....

4   I'm waiting for <u>my parents</u>.
      ....

5   Do <u>your exercises</u> now, please.
      ....

6   Fred wants to play with <u>my brother and me</u>.
      ....

Pairwork

Work with a partner.
Have short dialogues like the
ones in exercise 8.

8 Complete the sentences with the words in the box.

be	eat	forget
go (x2)	have (x2)	
invite	spend	~~visit~~

Writing

Think about the weekend.
Write ten suggestions with
Let's or *Let's not.*

Eg   *Let's ......visit...... our cousins later.*
      OK, but don't ......forget...... to buy them a present!

1   Let's .... shopping today.
      OK, but don't .... a lot of money.

2   Let's .... a party this evening.
      OK, but don't .... hundreds of people!

3   Let's .... pizza for supper.
      OK, but don't .... too much!

4   Let's .... for a walk by the sea!
      OK, but don't .... late for lunch.

....
....
....
....
....
....
....
....
....
....

 Past Simple: To Be

Past Simple: To Be

Affirmative	Negative	Question
I was	I was not (wasn't)	Was I?
you were	you were not (weren't)	Were you?
he was	he was not (wasn't)	Was he?
she was	she was not (wasn't)	Was she?
it was	it was not (wasn't)	Was it?
we were	we were not (weren't)	Were we?
you were	you were not (weren't)	Were you?
they were	they were not (weren't)	Were they?

Short answers

Yes, I was.	No, I wasn't.
Yes, you were.	No, you weren't.
Yes, he was.	No, he wasn't.
Yes, she was.	No, she wasn't.
Yes, it was.	No, it wasn't.
Yes, we were.	No, we weren't.
Yes, you were.	No, you weren't.
Yes, they were.	No, they weren't

The Past Simple of the verb *to be* is *was/were*.
He was at work this morning.
We were at the beach yesterday.

The negative is formed by putting the word *not* after the verb. The short form is *wasn't/weren't*.
I wasn't at a football match last Saturday.

The question is formed by changing the word order of the subject and the verb.
Were you awake all night?

Notes

We use time expressions such as *yesterday, yesterday morning, last Saturday, last week,* etc with the Past Simple. These expressions usually go at the beginning or end of a sentence.

Complete the sentences with **was** or **were**.

Eg I .....*was*..... in London yesterday.

1 They .... late for work this morning.

2 Jim .... at a nice hotel last year.

3 Tonic .... at home.

4 We .... with some friends last Saturday.

5 You .... tired last night.

6 I .... at the gym yesterday.

7 Last summer, Mum and Dad .... in England.

8 Martha Divine .... in the pool yesterday.

THINK
ABOUT IT!

*There is no affirmative short form for **to be** in the Past Simple.*

3
Complete the questions with **was** or **were** and write answers.

Eg ....*Were*......... they with you at the hotel? ✗
No, they weren't.

1 .... you at home on Sunday evening? ✓
    ....

2 .... Jim on holiday last August? ✓
    ....

3 .... your parents at the concert on Saturday? ✗
    ....

4 .... the bag under the desk? ✓
    ....

5 .... the apples in the bag? ✓
    ....

6 .... I late for the lesson? ✗
    ....

2
Make the sentences negative.

Eg *They were at home this morning.*
They weren't at home this morning.

1 My friend was at school today.
   ....

2 You were well yesterday.
   ....

3 I was on the bus this afternoon.
   ....

4 Martha Divine was happy last month.
   ....

5 We were very busy last summer.
   ....

6 They were at work on Monday.
   ....

7 The books were on the table.
   ....

8 The cake was in the fridge.
   ....

4
Write the words in the correct order.

Eg they / school / yesterday / were / at / ?
Were they at school yesterday?

1 garden / wasn't / the / yesterday / she / in
   ....

2 home / were / my mum / and I / all day / at
   ....

3 was / Mum / kitchen / the / in
   ....

4 park / boys / the / the / were / at / ?
   ....

5 in / the / wasn't / teacher / room / the
   ....

6 bed / Tonic / on / was / the / ?
   ....

7 children / last night / happy / the / weren't /
   ....

8 the / good / was / weather / yesterday / ?
   ....

59

Write questions and answers.

Eg *the books / on the bed / ? (on the table)*
Were the books on the bed?
No, they weren't. They were on the table.

I the boys / at school / last week / ? (at home)
....
....

2 Martha Divine / in a plane / ? (in a jeep)
....
....

3 Tonic / sad / yesterday / ? (happy)
....
....

4 Jim / in the shower / last night / ? (in the bath)
....
....

5 the girls / in the house / yesterday / ? (in the garden)
....
....

6

Complete the text with **was, wasn't, were** or **weren't**.

Last Saturday, I (Eg) ......*was*..... at my friend Paul's house. His sister (1) .... there too but his brother (2) .... there. He (3) .... at work. The weather (4) .... very good that day – it (5) .... cold and wet.

Pauls' room (6) .... tidy – like mine! Some CDs (7) .... on his desk and all his books (8) .... on the floor! His mum and dad (9) .... at home. They (10) .... at his aunt's house.

At nine o'clock, it (11) .... time to go home. I (12) .... happy, but tired.

There Was / There Were

Affirmative	Negative	Question
there was there were	there was not (there wasn't) there were not (there weren't)	Was there? Were there?

Short answers	
Yes, there was. Yes, there were.	No, there wasn't. No, there weren't.

We use *there was* and *there were* to talk or ask about what existed when we are describing something in the past.
There was a sailing boat on the sea.
There were lots of people at the party.

Complete the sentences with **there was / there were**.

Eg ....*There was*........ a book on the table. ✓
1 .... a lot of flowers in the garden. ✗
2 .... a cat in the kitchen?
3 .... three bones in Tonic's bowl. ✓
4 .... eggs in the fridge?
5 .... a cream cake in the fridge. ✓
6 .... a boat on the sea. ✗
7 .... people in the building. ✓
8 .... big trees in the garden?

Pairwork

Work with a partner. Take turns to ask and answer the following questions:

- Where were you last summer?
- Were you by the sea?
- Were you in the mountains?
- Were you in a village?

- Was your best friend with you?
- Were you with your family?
- Were you happy there?
- Was the weather good?

Writing

Write a paragraph for your class magazine about last summer.
Use the questions above to help you.

Review 3 (Units 9–12)

1 Complete the sentences with the Present Simple.

Eg   She ......*doesn't play*...... volleyball every day. (not play)

1   They .... tennis lessons on Saturdays. (not have)

2   She .... milk. (not like)

3   .... he .... English? (speak)

4   They .... by plane. (always / travel)

5   We .... very cold weather. (not like)

6   .... you .... that girl over there? (you / know)

7   She .... very slowly. (run)

8   .... they .... in London? (live)

2 Complete the sentences with the Present Continuous.

Eg   Look! They ......*are talking*...... to those awful people. (talk)

1   She .... the piano at the moment. (play)

2   Where is Mike? .... he .... his friend? (visit)

3   The students .... hard this year. (study)

4   I .... my homework, I ....
to music. (not do, listen)

5   .... they .... German this year? (learn)

6   She .... dinner with us tonight. (not have)

7   The children .... model aeroplanes. (make)

8   We .... in the park. (sit)

3 Complete the sentences with the Present Simple or Present Continuous.

Eg   She ......*never gets up*...... early on Saturdays. (never / get up)

1   They .... their friends at the weekend. (usually / see)

2   Barbara .... on holiday today. (go)

3   Uncle George .... me a present on my birthday. (always / give)

4   .... they .... to go to the museum every day? (want)

5   It's late and they .... the shop now. (close)

6   We .... on Saturdays. (never / work)

7   .... it .... at the moment? (rain)

8   Listen! The phone .... (ring)

Complete the sentences with **can** and the verbs in brackets.

Eg ....Can.......... she ....have........ a pizza this evening? (have)

1 .... I .... the film on TV tonight? (watch)

2 You .... now, the concert is starting. (not leave)

3 .... I .... your camera? (borrow)

4 You .... to your friend's house now. Your aunt is coming
to visit. (not go)

5 .... you .... Russian? (speak)

6 He .... to the party this weekend. (not come)

7 They .... me with the cooking for the party. (help)

8 I .... my watch. (not find)

Write questions with **can** and write answers.

Eg *you / speak French / ?*
Can you speak French?
Yes, I can.

1 we / have / wine with dinner / ? ✓

....

....

2 I / open the window / ? ✗

....

....

3 they / go to the cinema / ? ✓

....

....

4 he / come with us / ? ✗

....

....

5 she / swim / ? ✓

....

....

6 he / do those difficult maths problems / ? ✗

....

....

7 she / play the guitar / ? ✓

....

....

8 you / ride a horse / ? ✗

....

....

Complete the sentences with **must** and the verbs in brackets.

Eg *Students ....mustn't chew.... chewing gum in class. (not chew)*

1 I .... my umbrella. (not forget)

2 I .... my homework now. (do)

3 We .... now. It's getting late. (go)

4 .... you .... the house now? (clean)

5 She .... the six o'clock bus to the station. (catch)

6 We .... on the desks. (not draw)

7 They .... in the library. (not talk)

8 .... you .... that terrible noise? (make)

Match and make sentences.

Eg	Stand		a	your name on the test paper.	Eg	*Stand up.*
I	Open		b	*up.*	I	
2	Don't make		c	at page 34.	2	
3	Come		d	here.	3	
4	Look		e	quiet.	4	
5	Listen to		f	the window.	5	
6	Be		g	me.	6	
7	Write		h	a noise.	7	

Write sentences with **Let's** or **Let's not**.

Eg   play / Monopoly / tonight ✗
    Let's not play Monopoly tonight.

Eg   have / some spaghetti / for dinner ✓
    Let's have some spaghetti for dinner.

I   be / late / for school ✗

2   buy / a watch / for her birthday ✓

3   water / the plants ✓

4   watch / TV ✗

5   go / to the shops ✗

6   have / a drink ✓

7   phone / Uncle Ben ✓

8   clean / the house / today ✗

Complete the sentences with Object Pronouns.

Eg   Give ....*me*............ the book immediately! (I)

I   Let's give .... to Pat! (the photos)

2   I must visit .... tomorrow. (he)

3   I don't want .... now. (ice cream)

4   Can you see ....? (our friends)

5   The artist is painting .... now. (you and me)

6   Are you learning ....? (the new words)

7   Can I meet ....? (your friend's mother)

8   We all like .... (Jim and Tonic)

64

10 Complete the sentences with the correct form of **there was/were**.

Eg *There were* .... ten schoolchildren on the bus. ✓

1 .... a book on your desk?

2 .... any crisps for the party. ✗

3 .... some ducks on the pond. ✓

4 .... three taxis outside the station. ✓

5 .... any people in the sea?

6 .... any cars on the street. ✗

7 .... a good film on TV last night?

8 .... a table in the middle of the room. ✓

11 Complete the sentences with the Past Simple of **to be**.

Eg She .... *wasn't* .... well yesterday. ✗

1 We .... very tired last night. ✓

2 Dad .... at work on Thursday. ✗

3 The pens .... on the desk. ✓

4 He .... at home at lunchtime. ✗

5 The chocolate .... in the cupboard. ✓

6 We .... late for school yesterday. ✗

7 I .... with my friends all day. ✓

8 They .... at the office yesterday. ✗

12 Complete the questions with **was** or **were** and write answers.

Eg .... *Was* .... she at the restaurant? ✗
.... *No, she wasn't.* ....

1 .... the books in the bag? ✓
....

2 .... he late for the lesson? ✗
....

3 .... my parents at the meeting? ✗
....

4 .... you late for the bus? ✓
....

5 .... Gemma at home on Friday? ✗
....

6 .... you on holiday last July? ✓
....

7 .... the cat under the bed? ✗
....

8 .... your friends at the concert on Sunday? ✓
....

Past Simple Affirmative: Regular & Irregular Verbs

Past Simple Affirmative

Regular Verbs	Irregular Verbs
I worked	I went
you worked	you went
he worked	he went
she worked	she went
it worked	it went
we worked	we went
you worked	you went
they worked	they went

We use the Past Simple to talk about:

- things in the past which have finished.
  I went to work at 8 am.

- things in the past which were habits.
  Last year he cycled to university every day.

- things in the past which happened one after the other.
  She opened the front door, went inside and put her bag down in the hall.

We form the Past Simple affirmative of regular verbs by adding the -ed ending.
work ➡ worked

When the verb ends in -e, we add -d.
bake ➡ baked

When the verb ends in a consonant and -y, we take off the -y and add -ied.
carry ➡ carried

When the verb ends in a vowel and -y, we just add -ed.

stay → stayed

When the verb ends in a vowel and a consonant and that vowel is stressed, we double the last consonant and add -ed.

permit → permitted

When the verb ends in -l, we double the -l and add -ed.

cancel → cancelled

There are many irregular verbs in English. We do not form the Past Simple of these verbs by adding -ed. See the Irregular Verbs list on page 108.

1 Complete the sentences with the Past Simple.

Eg   We ....watched........ a good film on TV last night. (watch)

1   They .... all evening. (talk)
2   We .... by the river and then had supper. (walk)
3   Dad .... the car yesterday. (wash)
4   People .... at the camera. (smile)
5   Mrs Green .... a very nice meal for us. (cook)
6   I .... to leave the party early. (want)
7   She .... a lovely picture of the horse. (paint)
8   He .... to his favourite music all morning. (listen)

THINK ABOUT IT!

*We do not double the **n** in **listen** because we stress the first, not the second, syllable.*

2 Complete the table.

Verb	Past Simple
begin	began
break	
build	
come	
do	
drive	
fall	
find	
fly	
get	
know	
learn	
meet	
spend	
say	
think	

3 Complete the sentences with the Past Simple.

Eg   He ....lost........... his notebook yesterday. (lose)

1   They .... their grandmother to the station. (take)
2   Mum .... a chocolate cake for my birthday. (make)
3   Bob .... a new sports car last month. (buy)
4   The students .... quietly in the classroom. (sit)
5   I .... a letter to my cousin last night. (write)
6   We .... our homework very quickly after school. (do)
7   She .... to Peter's party with Michael. (come)
8   Jim .... loudly in the bath. (sing)

Ago

We use the word *ago* to talk about something that happened a number of years, minutes, days, etc in the past.
I bought this house two months ago.
He arrived ten minutes ago.
Harry went to bed three hours ago.

4 Write sentences with **ago**.

Eg *We bought the house in November.*
It is now December.
We bought the house one month ago.

1 He went there in March. It is now October.

....

2 She visited us in September. It is now February.

....

3 She was born in 1989.

....

5 Write the words in the correct order.

Eg *sent / yesterday / letter / the / he*
He sent the letter yesterday.

1 the / last / cinema / went / to / we / night

....

2 visited / two / us / ago / she / years

....

3 last / I / letter / a / long / wrote / night

....

4 my / flew / into / garden / birds / three

....

5 three / sandwiches / hour / ate / she / an / ago

....

6 friend / met / beach / I / on / a / the

....

7 teacher / spoke / quietly / to the children / the

....

8 yesterday / the / Mr Davis / left / office / early

....

6 Find the mistakes and write the sentences correctly.

Eg *He send me a red rose yesterday.*
He sent me a red rose yesterday.

1 I come to this school three years ago.

....

2 They were had a nice time yesterday.

....

3 He teach us French last year.

....

4 We went to the cinema before four days.

....

5 He break his leg ago a week.

....

4 She phoned us at eight o'clock. It is now nine o'clock.

....

5 We saw them last year.

....

6 I learnt to swim when I was seven. I am now fourteen.

....

7 Complete the sentences with the Past Simple. Use the words in the box.

ask	deliver	catch	have	open
start	walk	work		

Eg He ......*caught*...... a big fish this morning.

1 They .... lunch at one o'clock.
2 He .... home with his friends.
3 The children .... their presents quickly.
4 The rain .... after lunch.
5 The postman .... some letters.
6 The teacher .... a question.
7 I .... hard in the office all day.

68

8 Complete the text with the Past Simple.

One day last summer, Jim and Tonic (Eg) ....*visited*.... (visit) an old castle outside their town. The day (1) .... (begin) very well because it (2) .... (be) hot and sunny. Tonic (3) .... (take) his camera with him and Jim (4) .... (drive) them there in his car.

They (5) .... (spend) all day at the castle and they (6) .... (learn) a lot about its history. At lunchtime, they (7) .... (sit) on the grass and (8) .... (have) a picnic. At the castle shop, Tonic (9) .... (buy) a postcard and Jim (10) .... (get) an ice cream. It (11) .... (be) a really nice day out!

9 Complete the sentences with the Past Simple. Use the words in the box.

see	fail	fly	drive	study	meet
like	shout	look	play	wash	

Eg   She ....*fell*........ off her chair yesterday.

1   The children .... in the garden all day.
2   He .... a plane in the sky.
3   He .... his car to the petrol station.
4   They .... from Sydney to Paris last year.
5   We .... our friends in the park at lunchtime.
6   I .... my face and went to bed.
7   We .... the food at your party. It was great.
8   She .... English and French at university.
9   She .... in the mirror and smiled.
10   He .... for help when he saw the knife.

Pairwork

Work with a partner. Talk about what you did last weekend. Start like this:
On Saturday, I ....

Writing

Write a postcard to a friend about a trip you went on. Tell him/her:

- where you went.
- who you went with.
- how you went there.
- what you saw.
- what you ate.
- what you did.

....
....
....
....
....
....
....
....
....
....
....

Past Simple Negative & Question

Past Simple Negative and Question

Affirmative	Negative	Question
I worked	I did not (didn't) work	Did I work?
you worked	you did not (didn't) work	Did you work?
he worked	he did not (didn't) work	Did he work?
she worked	she did not (didn't) work	Did she work?
it worked	it did not (didn't) work	Did it work?
we worked	we did not (didn't) work	Did we work?
you worked	you did not (didn't) work	Did you work?
they worked	they did not (didn't) work	Did they work?

Short answers

Yes, I did.	No, I didn't.
Yes, you did.	No, you didn't.
Yes, he did.	No, he didn't.
Yes, she did.	No, she didn't.
Yes, it did.	No, it didn't.
Yes, we did.	No, we didn't.
Yes, you did.	No, you didn't.
Yes, they did.	No, they didn't.

The negative of the Past Simple (regular and irregular verbs) is formed with the auxiliary verb *did*, the word *not* and the bare infinitive.
The train didn't arrive on time.

The question form of the Past Simple (regular and irregular verbs) is formed with *did* and the bare infinitive.
Did the train arrive on time?

1 Complete the sentences with the negative form of the Past Simple.

Eg I ....*didn't like*...................... the horror film. (like)

1 They .... at the hotel because it was full. (stay)
2 The car .... at the traffic lights. (stop)
3 Our friends .... early enough for lunch. (arrive)
4 She .... the balcony yesterday. (wash)
5 Jim and Tonic .... at all the photos. (look)
6 Pete .... football yesterday. (play)
7 The children .... TV last night. (watch)
8 I .... to work this morning. (walk)

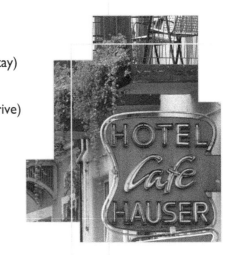

2 Complete the questions with the Past Simple.

Eg ....*Did you clean*.................. the dining room? (you / clean)

1 .... hard yesterday? (they / study)
2 .... all our friends to the party? (you / invite)
3 .... with the shopping? (she / help)
4 .... to the teacher? (the student / talk)
5 .... your teeth this morning? (you / brush)
6 .... all the food? (we / finish)
7 .... by plane or by boat? (they / travel)
8 .... when he cut his foot? (the boy / cry)

3 Make the sentences negative.

Eg *Mum made a pizza yesterday.*
...................*Mum didn't make a pizza yesterday.*...................

1 I wrote a letter to my uncle.
....

2 She broke all the glasses.
....

3 Tonic dug a hole in the garden.
....

4 They came to work late yesterday.
....

5 He did all his homework yesterday.
....

THINK ABOUT IT!

Be careful with the verb **do**:
Affirmative: I **did** my homework.
Negative: I **didn't do** my homework.
Question: **Did** you **do** your homework?

6 We met our friends at the restaurant.
....

7 They built a house near the sea.
....

8 They gave me the keys.
....

71

4 Write questions.

Eg *John became very angry.*
   Did John become very angry?

1 The ball fell in the river.
   ....

2 She found her watch.
   ....

3 They flew to Paris.
   ....

4 You thought about it carefully.
   ....

5 She made a chocolate cake this afternoon.
   ....

6 You sang in the concert.
   ....

7 Our team won the match.
   ....

8 They left the meeting early.
   ....

5 Write questions for the answers.

Eg *Did she like her presents?*

   Yes, she liked her presents.

1 ....
   Yes, he went to America.

2 ....
   Yes, they had a nice time.

3 ....
   No, I didn't do any work.

4 ....
   Yes, she wrote a good story.

5 ....
   No, he didn't drive there.

6 ....
   Yes, they visited the castle.

7 ....
   Yes, he played football yesterday.

8 ....
   No, I didn't run round the park.

Write the words in the correct order.

Eg *go / last / to / the / did / night / they / cinema / ?*
.....*Did they go to the cinema last night?*..

1 didn't / he / you / see / there
....

2 do / homework / she / her / did / ?
....

3 speak / her / to / I / didn't
....

4 rain / didn't / it / yesterday
....

5 door / lock / didn't / you / the
....

6 you / car / did / wash / the / ?
....

Pairwork

Work with a partner. Take turns to ask and answer the following questions about last weekend:

- Did you wake up early on Saturday morning?
- Did you have a big breakfast?
- Did you go shopping?
- Did you stay at home on Saturday afternoon?
- Did you enjoy yourself on Saturday evening?
- Did you see your friends?
- Did you wake up early on Sunday morning?
- Did you do anything interesting on Sunday?
- Did you spend the day with your family?
- Did you go to bed early on Sunday?

Writing

Write ten things you didn't do when you were on holiday, but that you wanted to do.

Some, Any, No, Every

Some, Any, No

We use the word *some* before a noun in an affirmative sentence to say that something exists.
There's some juice in the fridge.
There are some magazines in my room.

We use the word *any* in negative sentences and questions to say that something doesn't exist or to ask if something exists.
He hasn't got any letters today.
Are there any eggs in the fridge?

We use the word *no* with an affirmative verb to make a sentence negative in meaning.
There are no people on the train.
(There aren't any people on the train.)

Notes
We can use the word *some* in questions when we are asking for something or offering something.
Can I have some new boots, please?
Can I get you some more coffee?

1 Complete the sentences with **some** or **any**.

Eg We *don't need* ....*any*.... *biscuits.*

1 The farmers need .... rain. It's very hot and dry.
2 There aren't .... crisps on the table.
3 Have you got .... money?
4 Can I have .... water, please?
5 We haven't got .... onions to make onion soup.
6 I can see .... children in the street.
7 We haven't got .... pets.
8 Are there .... shops near your home?

Complete the sentences with **any** or **no**.

Eg *There are .... children in the park today.*

1 I haven't got .... money in my purse.

2 Did you buy .... tickets for the cinema?

3 There was .... rain all summer.

4 There is .... wine in the bottle.

5 There wasn't .... noise in the classroom.

6 He hasn't got .... homework tonight.

7 There are .... taxis today.

8 Tonic can't find .... bones.

Someone, Anyone, No one, Everyone

People	Things	Places
someone/somebody	something	somewhere
anyone/anybody	anything	anywhere
no one/nobody	nothing	nowhere
everyone/everybody	everything	everywhere

We usually use the words that begin with *some-* in affirmative sentences.

We use the words *someone* and *somebody* to talk about one unspecified person. There is no difference between *someone* and *somebody*.
Someone telephoned you this morning.

We use the word *something* to talk about one unspecified thing.
There's something in my boot.

We use the word *somewhere* to talk about one unspecified place.
I left my sunglasses somewhere!

We use the words *anyone/anybody*, *anything* and *anywhere* to talk about one unspecified person, thing or place. We usually use the words that begin with *any-* in negative sentences and questions.
There wasn't anybody at home.
Is there anyone here?
I can't find anything to wear.

We use the words *no-one/nobody*, *nothing* and *nowhere* in affirmative sentences when the verb is affirmative but the meaning of the sentence is negative.
No-one heard him.
I ate nothing all morning.
There is nowhere for me to sit.

We use the words *everyone/everybody*, *everything* and *everywhere* to talk about all the people, things or places.

When the words *everyone/everybody* and *everything* are the subjects of a sentence, they are followed by a verb in the third person singular.

Everyone was at the party.
I paid for everything.
I've looked everywhere for my glasses!

3 Complete the sentences with **someone, anyone** or **everyone**.

Eg *There's ....someone.......... at the door.*

1 They asked .... to the party. The whole neighbourhood came!

2 I can't see .... outside. It's very dark!

3 Can .... help me, please?

4 There wasn't .... at school when I got there.

5 .... in the class got good marks in the exam. The teacher was pleased.

6 What's that noise? .... is shouting in the street.

THINK ABOUT IT!

*We can use **some** and words with **some** in questions to offer something to someone or to ask for something.*

4 Rewrite the sentences using the word given. Use between two and five words.

Eg *There isn't anyone on the bus.* **nobody**
There ....is nobody.......... on the bus.

1 There is nothing I can do about your problem. **anything**
There .... I can do about your problem.

2 There isn't anywhere we can hide. **nowhere**
There .... we can hide.

3 There was nothing good on television last night. **anything**
There .... good on television last night.

4 There wasn't anybody in the room. **nobody**
There .... in the room.

5 There is no information about the subject on the Internet. **any**
There .... about the subject on the Internet.

THINK ABOUT IT!

*We cannot use **everyone** or **everybody** after There is.*

76

Eg *I know .... about chess, but not much.*
   a *anything*   **b** *everything*   **c** *something*

1 I can't find my pen. It isn't .... in the house.
   a nowhere   **b** anywhere   **c** somewhere

2 I like .... in that clothes shop!
   a anything   **b** everywhere   **c** everything

3 I know my keys are .... in the house!
   a somewhere   **b** anywhere   **c** everywhere

4 Did you see .... on the floor?
   a nothing   **b** everywhere   **c** anything

5 There is .... in the garden.
   a somebody   **b** anybody   **c** everybody

6 We went .... last weekend.
   a anywhere   **b** nowhere   **c** anybody

Pairwork

Work with a partner. Make up a ghost story, using words from this unit.

Writing

Write a ghost story or a mystery story. Use words from this unit.

....
....
....
....
....
....
....
....
....
....

Countable & Uncountable Nouns & Quantifiers

Countable and Uncountable Nouns

Countable Nouns	Uncountable Nouns
bottle	bread
CD	cheese
chair	fish
computer	food
invitation	meat
knife	milk
notebook	money
programme	spaghetti
sandwich	tea
woman	water

Nouns that we can count and that we can use in the plural are called countable nouns. When the subject of a sentence is in the plural, the verb must also be in the plural.
There are three secretaries in the office.
They have got five dogs.

Nouns that we cannot count and that do not have plurals are called uncountable nouns. We do not use *a* and *an* with uncountable nouns. When the subject of a sentence is an uncountable noun, the verb must be in the singular.
The food was delicious.
The bread is fresh.

We can use other words with uncountable nouns so that we know how much we have, such as *a bottle of* (wine), *a slice of* (bread), *a piece of* (cheese), *a glass of* (milk), *a kilo of* (butter), *a plate of* (spaghetti), etc.

We can use the word *some* in front of countable and uncountable nouns in affirmative sentences.
There are some eggs in the box.
There is some wine in the bottle.

We can use the word *any* in front of countable and uncountable nouns in negative sentences and questions.
There aren't any dogs in the park.
Is there any milk left?

We can use the word *no* in front of countable and uncountable nouns with an affirmative verb to give a sentence a negative meaning.
There are no books on the shelf.
There is no soap in the bathroom.

---

1 Complete the sentences with **a, an** or **some**.

Eg   *There were* .... *chairs around the table.*

1   There's .... big blue bowl on the table.

2   There are .... vegetables in the fridge.

3   I want to buy .... green apples from the supermarket.

4   Jim's got .... old red jacket in his cupboard.

5   I must get .... dog food for Tonic!

6   You made .... mistake in this exercise.

7   We met .... interesting people at the beach.

8   She wants to be .... actress.

THINK ABOUT IT!

We do not use a or an with Uncountable Nouns.

---

2 Choose the correct answer.

Eg   Is / Are *there any milk in the fridge?*

1   *Is / Are there any cold water in the fridge?*

2   The milk *is / are* not fresh. We must get some more.

3   There *is / are* six hundred people in this building.

4   This cheese *is / are* awful! I can't eat it.

5   There *isn't / aren't* any clothes on the bed.

6   The food in this restaurant *is / are* really excellent!

7   *Is / Are* the wine from France?

8   The strawberries *is / are* sweet and juicy.

3

Match and make phrases. Then write them under the pictures.

Eg	*a loaf of*	a	rice
1	a carton of	b	coffee
2	a jar of	c	chocolate
3	a packet of	d	honey
4	a bottle of	e	*bread*
5	a cup of	f	cheese
6	a bar of	g	water
7	a piece of	h	milk

Eg  *a loaf of bread*

1 ....

2 ....

3 ....

4 ....

5 ....

6 ....

7 ....

Much and Many

We use *much* with uncountable nouns in negative sentences and questions.
He doesn't earn much money.
Have you got much work this week?

We use the word *many* with countable nouns in negative sentences and questions.
There aren't many customers in the shop.
Have you got many books about horses?

When we ask about quantity, we use *How much?* for uncountable nouns and *How many?* for countable nouns.
How much bread is there?
How many people were at the party?

4

Complete the sentences with **much** or **many**.

Eg Was there ......*much*...... milk in the bottle?

1 We don't have .... petrol left.

2 Are there .... colourful birds in Africa?

3 He doesn't have .... furniture in his house.

4 There isn't .... soup left for me!

5 Has he got .... friends at school?

6 There aren't .... flowers in the garden.

7 Were there .... loaves of bread on the shelf?

8 There isn't .... cheese on his pizza.

80

Complete the questions with **much** or **many**.

Eg How ....*much*.......... coffee have you got?

1 How .... cheese do you want?
2 How .... plates are there in the cupboard?
3 How .... CDs have they got?
4 How .... water is there in the sea?
5 How .... books did you borrow?
6 How .... salt did you put in the soup?
7 How .... mistakes did you make?
8 How .... sugar is there in this tea?

A Little, A Few, A Lot / Lots (Of)

We use a *little* with uncountable nouns when we want to say that a small amount of something exists. It has a positive meaning.
Can I have something to eat?
Yes, there's a little cake left on the table.

We use *a few* with countable nouns when we want to say that a small number of something exists. It has a positive meaning.
There are a few tickets left for the concert.

We use *a lot (of)* and *lots (of)* with countable nouns and uncountable nouns in affirmative and negative sentences and in questions.
We have got a lot of cousins.
There are lots of hotels in Spain.
Has he got lots of friends?
They haven't got a lot of money.

Complete the sentences with **a few** or **a little**.

Eg I've got ....*a few*........ very good friends.

1 She made .... mistakes in the test.
2 There is .... orange juice in the jug.
3 Can I have .... water, please?
4 They saw .... good films last year.
5 I've got .... money in my purse.
6 Barbara wants .... new clothes this summer.
7 We met .... interesting people at the party.
8 The soup needs .... salt.

Choose the correct answer.

Eg *There isn't ..... meat in the freezer.*
   a *many*   **(b)** *much*   **c** *a few*

1 She's got ..... nice clothes.
   a a few   **b** much   **c** a little

2 How ..... petrol is in the car? Do we need to buy any?
   a many   **b** much   **c** a little

3 He hasn't got ..... friends.
   a many   **b** much   **c** lots

4 You've got ..... CDs!
   a much   **b** lots of   **c** a little

5 I want ..... salt and pepper on my food.
   a much   **b** a little   **c** many

6 We took ..... nice books out of the library.
   a a little   **b** lots   **c** a few

7 Are there ..... interesting places near your house?
   a many   **b** much   **c** a little

8 Is there ..... milk in the jug?
   a many   **b** lots   **c** much

Complete the text with the words from the box.

| a | any | *few* | lots | piece |
| little | much | some (x3) | | |

Last Saturday, Vicky and her family went to a restaurant because it was her mother's birthday. They went early and there were only a (Eg) .....*few*...... people there. Vicky didn't want (1) .... food because she wasn't very hungry. But her father was very hungry! He ordered (2) .... of chips and (3) .... bowl of salad. Then he ate a large (4) .... of meat. Vicky's mum ordered (5) .... fish. Vicky didn't want (6) .... meat or fish, so she ordered (7) .... onion soup — her favourite! Vicky's mum and dad drank a (8) .... wine but Vicky had (9) .... lemonade. Then they all wished her mum a very Happy Birthday!

any	few	how	little	lot
lots	many	much	some

Eg   *There isn't* ....*any*............ *butter in the fridge.*

1   How .... sugar do you need?

2   He's got .... sweets in his bag.

3   They haven't got .... books to read.

4   I've got a .... of things to do today.

5   There are only a .... bananas on the table.

6   .... much ice cream do we need?

7   She wants a .... milk in her coffee.

8   They did .... of interesting things on holiday.

Pairwork

Work with a partner. Take turns to ask and answer questions about
what you *have got* or *haven't got*. Here are some ideas:

- CDs
- books
- friends
- brothers/sisters
- bags
- key rings
- money
- pets

Writing

Write a short paragraph about what you *have got* and what *you haven't got*.
Use words you have learnt in this unit.

....
....
....
....
....
....
....
....
....

Review 4 (Units 13–16)

1

Complete the sentences with the Past Simple.

Eg   We ....*listened*........ to some great music last night. *(listen)*

1   His wife .... a special meal for his birthday. *(prepare)*

2   I .... to cook spaghetti but it wasn't very good! *(try)*

3   The artist .... pictures of the countryside. *(paint)*

4   The young man .... my heavy shopping for me. *(carry)*

5   They .... on the phone all evening. *(talk)*

6   We .... through the old part of the village. *(walk)*

7   I .... the house yesterday. *(clean)*

8   They .... over the mountains on donkeys. *(travel)*

2   Complete the chart.

Verbs	Past Simple
break	*broke*
catch	
dig	
draw	
drink	
eat	
fall	
get	
have	
know	
make	
sit	
speak	
spend	
take	
think	

3   Complete the sentences with the Past Simple.

Eg   I ....*came*........ home early last night. *(come)*

1   We .... our homework very quickly yesterday. *(do)*

2   I .... my keys yesterday. *(lose)*

3   My best friend .... in a concert yesterday. *(sing)*

4   They .... their friends to the airport. *(drive)*

5   I .... ill, so I stayed at home. *(feel)*

6   Bob .... a new sports car last month. *(buy)*

7   The students .... down everything the teacher said. *(write)*

8   She .... an e-mail to her friend this morning. *(send)*

4 Complete the sentences with the negative form of the Past Simple.

Eg   We ....*didn't look*.......... at all the photos. (look)

1   He .... to the shops this morning. (walk)

2   We .... a lot of mistakes yesterday. (make)

3   She .... a letter to her penfriend last weekend. (write)

4   My cousin .... basketball yesterday. (play)

5   I .... TV last night. (watch)

6   The cook .... a plate at lunchtime. (break)

7   We .... all the irregular verbs this morning. (learn)

8   My brother .... to Hawaii last January. (fly)

5 Complete the questions with the Past Simple.

Eg   ....*Did you think*.......... it was Monday today?

(you / think)

1   .... to Germany? (they / drive)

2   .... when she fell down?

(Donna / cry)

3   .... about her new job?

(you / know)

4   .... out of the window?

(the ball / fall)

5   .... all the pizza? (we / finish)

6   .... your hair this morning?

(you / brush)

7   .... your plane ticket?

(you / find)

8   .... to New York? (they / fly)

6 Write sentences and questions with the Past Simple.

Eg   *we / not go to the cinema / last week*
     We didn't go to the cinema last week.
     ....

1   he / buy flowers / for his mother / ?
    ....

2   I / not spend time / with my friends
    ....

3   you / walk to work / yesterday / ?
    ....

4   they / fly to London / last night / ?
    ....

5   she / not wash her car / yesterday
    ....

6   it / rain in Spain / last week / ?
    ....

7   we / not watch TV / last night
    ....

8   you / speak to David / last weekend / ?
    ....

85

7

Complete the sentences with **some** or **any**.

Eg   *I don't want ....any........ food, thank you.*

1   I can see .... birds in the garden.
2   We don't have .... bread.
3   Are there .... parks where you live?
4   We don't need .... help.
5   We want .... good weather.
6   There aren't .... glasses on the table.
7   Have you got .... money?
8   Here are .... presents for you.

8

Complete the sentences with **any** or **no**.

Eg   *There wasn't ....any........ wine for the party.*

1   He doesn't have .... work this evening.
2   There are .... buses today.
3   He can't find .... pencils.
4   There are .... biscuits in the tin.
5   I haven't got .... coffee.
6   Did you buy .... clothes for the trip?
7   There wasn't .... snow all winter.
8   There is .... milk in the bottle.

9

Complete the sentences with **someone**, **anyone** or **everyone**.

Eg   *There wasn't ....anyone........ at the office early this morning.*

1   .... in the class went to the zoo. We had a lovely time.
2   I need .... to help me. Ian, can you help?
3   There's .... at the door. Can you open it, please?
4   When the bell rang, ... went home.
5   Hello? Is there .... there?
6   Can .... do the washing up, please?
7   .... was happy when they heard the good news.
8   I didn't know .... at first, but I soon made friends.

10

Choose the correct answer.

Eg *There were .... people at the party.*
    a much   *b any*   ⓒ *a lot of*

I   We have .... good CDs to listen to.
    a lots   **b** much   **c** lots of

2   Is there .... ice cream in the freezer?
    a many   **b** a lot   **c** much

3   How .... pairs of shoes has she got?
    a many   **b** any   **c** much

4   We haven't got .... bread.
    a many   **b** much   **c** a few

5   He's got .... good friends.
    a any   **b** a few   **c** lots

6   There are .... exercises in this book.
    a a little   **b** much   **c** a lot of

7   He hasn't got .... money.
    a many   **b** much   **c** some

8   Are there .... interesting old buildings
    in your town?
    a any   **b** much   **c** some

11

Put the words in the correct part of the chart.

biscuit   egg   fork   honey   knife   money   newspaper   orange
    orange juice   potato   salt   sandwich   spaghetti   sugar   water   wine

Countable Nouns	Uncountable Nouns
biscuit	*honey*

12

Match

Eg *a carton of*   a   honey
I   a loaf of   b   bread
2   a packet of   c   cake
3   a can of   d   chocolate
4   a bottle of   e   *yoghurt*
5   a cup of   f   cola
6   a bar of   g   rice
7   a jar of   h   wine
8   a piece of   i   coffee

Comparison of Adjectives

Comparative

We use the comparative form to compare two people, animals or things. We often use the word *than* after the comparative form.
He's taller than me.
This chair is more expensive than the other chair.

To make the comparative form of adjectives with one syllable, we add the ending *-er*.
tall → *taller*

When the adjective ends in *-e*, we just add *-r*.
late → *later*

When the adjective ends in a vowel and a consonant, we double the last consonant and add *-er*.
fit → *fitter*

When an adjective ends in *-y*, we take off the *-y* and add *-ier*.
early → *earlier*

Sometimes we use the word *more* with two-syllable adjectives to make the comparative form.
famous → *more famous*

Some two-syllable adjectives have two comparative forms.
simple → *simpler/more simple*
clever → *cleverer/more clever*
polite → *politer/more polite*

We use the word *more* to make the comparative form of adjectives with three or more syllables.
confusing → *more confusing*

Some adjectives are irregular and do not follow these rules.
good → *better*   *bad* → *worse*

1 Complete the sentences with the Comparative form.

Eg *Their house is ....bigger........... than ours. (big)*

1 This ferry is .... than the cruise ship. (slow)

2 Her children are .... than other children. (polite)

3 She's .... than her daughter. (beautiful)

4 The football fans were .... than the basketball fans. (noisy)

5 Spain is .... than England. (warm)

6 My dog is .... than yours. (fat)

7 A motorbike is .... than a car. (dangerous)

8 This suitcase is .... than that one. (heavy)

Superlative

We use the superlative form to compare more than two people, animals or things. We often use a phrase beginning with *in* or *of* to continue the sentence.
She's the most beautiful girl in the school!
She's the tallest of all her sisters.

To make the superlative form of adjectives with one syllable, we add the ending -*est*. We use the word *the* before the adjective in its superlative form.
tall → *the tallest*

When the adjective ends in -*e*, we just add -*st*.
late → *the latest*

When the adjective ends in a vowel and a consonant, we double the last consonant and add -*est*.
fit → *the fittest*

When an adjective ends in -*y*, we take off the -*y* and add -*iest*.
happy → *happiest*

Sometimes we use *the most* with a two-syllable adjective to make the superlative form.
famous → *the most famous*

Some two-syllable adjectives have two superlative forms.
simple → *the simplest/the most simple*
clever → *the cleverest/the most clever*
polite → *the politest/the most polite*

We use the word *most* to make the superlative form of adjectives with three or more syllables.
confusing → *the most confusing*

Some adjectives are irregular and do not follow these rules.
good → *the best*
bad → *the worst*

Notes
The words *much, many, a lot (of), a little* and *a few* also have comparative and superlative forms.

much	→	more	→	the most
many	→	more	→	the most
a lot (of)	→	more	→	the most
lots (of)	→	more	→	the most
a little	→	less	→	the least
a few	→	fewer	→	the fewest

2 Complete the sentences with the Superlative form.

Eg   She is ....*the nicest*.............. person I know. (nice)

1   This is .... day in the week. (bad)

2   Her project was .... one in the class. (interesting)

3   At our restaurant you can eat .... fish in the country! (tasty)

4   Those exercises are .... of all. (difficult)

5   She's .... in the family. (old)

6   My brother is .... of all his friends. (tall)

7   Today is .... day of the year. (hot)

8   .... ride at the fair is the Big Wheel. (exciting)

as ... as

We can also use (not) as ... as to compare two people, animals or things.

We use as ... as when the two people, animals or things are the same.
He is as tall as his father.

We use not as ... as when they are different.
This book isn't as good as that book.

3 Write sentences using **as ... as** or **not as ... as**.

Eg   *This mountain is 902 metres. That mountain is 902 metres. (high)*
This mountain is ....*as high as*.............. *that mountain.*

1   The dog is fifteen kilos. The cat is six kilos. (heavy)
The cat is .... the dog.

2   Aunt Belle is sixty-one years old. Aunt Gertrude is sixty-one years old. (old)
Aunt Belle is .... Aunt Gertrude.

3   The kitchen is five metres long. The sitting room is seven metres long. (long)
The kitchen is .... the sitting room.

4   David got 9 marks for his composition. Nancy got 9 marks for her composition. (good)
Nancy's composition was .... David's.

5   Mike can lift 48 kilos. Brian can lift 55 kilos. (strong)
Mike is .... Brian.

4 Write the words in the correct order.

Eg   shorter / friends / she / than / is / her
She is shorter than her friends.

1   at school / Tony / than / brother / his / is / better
....
....

2   more / history / interesting / than / is / geography
....
....

3   the / is / player / the / he / best / team / in
....
....

4   is / this / as / ours / as / flat / large
....
....

5   exercise / than / is / the / easier / others / this
....
....

6   in / popular / she / the USA / the / singer / is / most
....
....

90

5 Complete the sentences with one word in each gap.

Eg   He's ......*the*...... best student ......*in*...... the class.

1   She's more intelligent .... her sister.
2   The maths problems aren't ....
    difficult as you think.
3   This is .... best day of my life!
4   *The Lord of the Rings* is the ....
    interesting book in the world!
5   He is .... as friendly as his brother.
6   He's the most famous film star ....
    the world.

Pairwork

Work with a partner. Look at the three photographs of holiday places with your partner and compare them. Use these words.

- beautiful
- boring
- cheap
- cold
- exciting
- expensive
- few
- hot
- many
- ugly

6 Read and complete with the Comparative or Superlative form.

There's a boy in my village called Tom. He's (Eg) ......*older*...... (old) than I am and he lives near me. His house is (1) .... (big) than ours and it's got a swimming pool.

Tom is (2) .... (clever) boy in the village and he's also (3) .... (funny)! He loves jokes and playing tricks on people. His mum makes (4) .... (good) cakes in the village and Tom eats (5) .... (many) cakes than anybody else!

Tom is (6) .... (good) than me at swimming but I run (7) .... (fast) than he does! Tom has got lots of friends because he's (8) .... (popular) boy in the village.

Writing

Find three pictures of different places, people or animals and compare them. Write a short paragraph.

....
....
....
....
....
....
....
....
....

Be Going To & Future Simple

Be Going To

Affirmative	Negative	Question
I am (I'm) going to play	I am not (I'm not) going to play	Am I going to play?
you are (you're) going to play	you are not (you aren't) going to play	Are you going to play?
he is (he's) going to play	he is not (he isn't) going to play	Is he going to play?
she is (she's) going to play	she is not (she isn't) going to play	Is she going to play?
it is (it's) going to play	it is not (it isn't) going to play	Is it going to play?
we are (we're) going to play	we are not (we aren't) going to play	Are we going to play?
you are (you're) going to play	you are not (you aren't) going to play	Are you going to play?
they are (they're) going to play	they are not (they aren't) going to play	Are they going to play?

Short answers

Yes, I am.	No, I'm not.
Yes, you are.	No, you aren't.
Yes, he is.	No, he isn't.
Yes, she is.	No, she isn't.
Yes, it is.	No, it isn't.
Yes, we are.	No, we aren't.
Yes, you are.	No, you aren't.
Yes, they are.	No, they aren't.

We use *be going to* to talk about:

- future plans and arrangements.
  Tomorrow we're going to visit a museum.

- something we know is going to happen because we have evidence.
  Watch out! That glass is going to fall off the table!

We can use time expressions such as *soon, tomorrow, next week, this evening, in the morning, tonight, at the weekend, later on,* etc with *be going to.*
We're going to paint the sitting room at the weekend.

1 Complete the sentences with **be going to** and the words in brackets.

Eg He ...*is going to take*... his exam next Saturday. (take)

1 I .... a bath tonight. (have)
2 They .... us this summer. (not visit)
3 We .... out late this evening. (not stay)
4 Look at those black clouds! It ....! (rain)
5 I .... those letters now. (not write)
6 He .... his friend later. (phone)
7 .... the teacher .... us our test papers? (give)
8 I .... him anything. (not tell)

2 Complete the questions with **be going to** and write answers.

Eg ...*Are you going to watch*........... the film on TV? (you / watch) ✗
    ...*No, I'm not.*...

1 .... some ice cream? (he / buy) ✗
   ....

2 .... by boat? (they / travel) ✓
   ....

3 .... all those cakes? (you / eat) ✓
   ....

4 .... in the summer? (she / study) ✗
   ....

5 .... home? (you / walk) ✓
   ....

6 .... the piano tomorrow? (she / play) ✗
   ....

7 .... for us this evening? (he / cook) ✓
   ....

8 .... him soon? (they / visit) ✗
   ....

Future Simple

Affirmative	Negative	Question
I will (I'll) play	I will not (won't) play	Will I play?
you will (you'll) play	you will not (won't) play	Will you play?
he will (he'll) play	he will not (won't) play	Will he play?
she will (she'll) play	she will not (won't) play	Will she play?
it will (it'll) play	it will not (won't) play	Will it play?
we will (we'll) play	we will not (won't) play	Will we play?
you will (you'll) play	you will not (won't) play	Will you play?
they will (they'll) play	they will not (won't) play	Will they play?

Short answers

Yes, I will.	No, I won't.
Yes, you will.	No, you won't.
Yes, he will.	No, he won't.
Yes, she will.	No, she won't.
Yes, it will.	No, it won't.
Yes, we will.	No, we won't.
Yes, you will.	No, you won't.
Yes, they will.	No, they won't.

We use the Future Simple:

■ for predictions for the future.
You will have lots of children and a long, happy life.

■ for decisions made at the time of speaking or to offer help.
I'll carry that bag for you.

■ for promises, threats and warnings.
You'll fall out of that tree.
I won't be late. I promise.

■ to ask someone to do something for us.
Will you look after the children this weekend?

■ after I hope, I think, I'm sure, I bet, etc.
I hope you'll come and see us soon.

We can use time expressions such as *soon, tomorrow, next week, this evening, in the morning, tonight, at the weekend, later on,* etc with the Future Simple.
We will win the competition at the weekend.

3 Complete the questions with the Future Simple and write answers.

Eg *Will you buy* .... some bread, please? (you / buy) ✓
Yes, I will.
....

1 .... at home this evening? (he / be) ✗
....

2 .... me with these bags? (you / help) ✓
....

3 .... fifteen next year? (she / be) ✗
....

4 .... later? (it / rain) ✓
....

5 .... dinner with us tomorrow? (they / have) ✓
....

6 .... angry about the broken window? (your dad / be) ✗
....

7 .... better tomorrow, Doctor? (she / feel) ✓
....

8 .... for us tonight? (you / cook) ✗
....

4 Complete the sentences with the Future Simple.

Eg *I'm sure they ...... will be ...... very happy to see you. (be)*

1 I bet he .... the same job next year. (not have)

2 We .... you with the shopping today. (help)

3 She .... her marks until next week. (not know)

4 I .... him to the party. (not ask)

5 I know my friends .... me. (tell)

6 I .... you at nine o'clock in the morning. (meet)

7 The weather .... fine and sunny tomorrow. (be)

8 Mary .... all the food we need. (buy)

5 Read and complete with **be going to** or the Future Simple.

It is two days before Jim and Tonic's party ...

Jim: This afternoon, I (Eg) ...... am going to buy ...... (buy) some things from the supermarket, Tonic. What (1) .... (you / do)?

Tonic: Well, I think I (2) .... (go) to the cake shop and then I think I (3) .... (invite) some more friends. I'm sure we (4) .... (have) a great time on Saturday, Jim!

Jim: (5) .... (Martha Divine / come), Tonic?

Tonic: Yes, she is, so be careful! I hope you (6) .... (not splash) water over her again!

Jim: No, I won't Tonic. I promise I (7) .... (be) very good and I (8) .... (not do) anything silly!

Pairwork

Work with a partner. Take turns to ask and answer about your plans for the summer holidays. For example:

- Where are you going to go?
- How are you going to travel there?
- Who is going to come with you?
- What are you going to do?

Writing

Write a short article for your school magazine about a place you are going to visit in the summer. Say what you are going to do there.

....
....
....
....
....
....
....
....

Question Words

We use question words when we want more information than *Yes* or *No*.
'Did you enjoy the film?' *'Yes, I did.'*
'Why did you enjoy the film?' *'Because it was a great adventure story and my favourite actor was starring in it.'*

How
We use *how* to ask about the way someone does something or to ask about someone's health.
How are you?
How did he learn all those words?

We can use *how* with adjectives and adverbs.
How old are they?
How often did you see them last year?
How many T-shirts have you got?
How much salt did you put in the food?

Who
We use *who* to ask about people.
Who are they inviting to their party?

What
We use *what* to ask about things or actions.
What happened?

When
We use *when* to ask about time.
When do you want to leave?

Where
We use *where* to ask about place.
Where did you put my shoes?

Which
We use *which* to ask about one person or thing within a group of similar people or things.
Which girl told you the news?

Whose
We use *whose* to ask who something belongs to.
Whose horse will you ride?

Why
We use *why* to ask about the reason for something.
Why are you crying?

1

Tick the correct question, **a** or **b**.

Eg **a** What are you doing? ✓
b What you are doing?

1 **a** Where did he eat?
b Where he ate?

2 **a** Why you are reading?
b Why are you reading?

3 **a** What his name was?
b What was his name?

4 **a** What I can do?
b What can I do?

5 **a** What your address is?
b What is your address?

6 **a** When does the party begin?
b When the party begins?

2

Complete the questions with **how, how much, how many, how old** or **how often**.

Eg ......*How much*...... money do you need?
Not much.

1 .... does he play basketball?
Twice a week.

2 .... do these jeans cost?
£25.

3 .... did you do in the test?
Very well.

4 .... children have they got?
Four.

5 .... are you?
I'm fine.

6 .... is your little sister?
She's twelve.

THINK ABOUT IT!

*We use **How much?** in questions like **How much (money) does it cost?** and **How much paper have you got?***

Subject / Object Questions

Subject Questions	Object Questions
When the question word asks about the subject (the person, animal or thing that does the verb), then the verb stays in the affirmative form. *Who came to the party?* (Lots of people came to the party.) *Whose horse won the race?* (My horse won the race.)	When the question word asks about the object, then the verb changes to the question form. *What did you buy?* (I bought a new CD.) *Which book do you like?* (I like *The Hobbit*.)

Notes
Do not confuse *Whose?*, *Who's?* (Who is?) and *Who's got?* (Who has got?).
Whose car did you buy? (I bought Gary's car.)
Who's that lady over there? (She's my father's secretary.)
Who's got a brother? (I've got a brother.)

3

Choose the correct answer.

Eg Who wants / does want to come with me?

1 Who *do you want* / *you want* to see?
2 Who *does like* / *likes* ice cream?
3 Who *opened* / *did open* the door?
4 Who *is he having* / *is having* a party?
5 Who *you are* / *are you*?
6 Who *did run* / *ran* very fast in the race?

97

4

Complete the questions with **Whose** or **Who's**.

Eg ...*Whose*.... pencil is this?

1 .... got a black pen?

2 .... at the front door?

3 .... mobile phone is ringing?

4 .... shoes are in the kitchen?

5 .... got a Porsche?

6 .... the most popular singer in your country?

5

Complete the questions with the words from the box.

How	What	When(x2)	Where
Who	Whose	Which	Why

Eg ...*When*.... are you going on holiday?

1 .... old is your brother?

2 .... boots are you going to buy?

3 .... personal stereo is this?

4 .... are you opening the window?

5 .... is he talking about?

6 .... are we going home?

7 .... are you going?

8 .... is that woman next to your mother?

6

Choose the correct answer.

Eg *Which programme* do you like / you like *best?*

1 Which student *did finish / finished* all the exercises first?

2 Which book *did you read / you read* last weekend?

3 Which machine *does work / works* well?

4 Which pen *does write / writes* better?

5 Which pizza *did you order / you ordered?*

7

Match the questions with the answers.

Eg *Where is my bag?*

1 How old is your mother?

2 When did they arrive?

3 How did you get to the island?

4 Why are they so sad?

5 How many sisters have you got?

6 Who is that good-looking boy over there?

7 What time do you usually get up?

8 How much water is there in the bottle?

9 Whose bag is under the table?

10 Which T-shirt do you like?

a By ferry.

b Last night.

c Not much.

d *Behind you.*

e Three.

f My cousin, Robert.

g Forty-one years old.

h At seven o'clock.

i Because their dog is very ill.

j The black one.

k Rita's.

Write questions. The underlined words are the answers.

Eg I met Marcus <u>three years ago</u>.
When did you meet Marcus?

1 <u>Barbara</u> invited John to her party.
....

2 Barbara invited <u>John</u> to her party.
....

3 We go <u>to Italy</u> every summer.
....

4 We went to the USA <u>last summer</u>.
....

5 I didn't like the film <u>because it was boring</u>.
....

6 <u>Georgia's</u> composition was the best in the class.
....

Pairwork

Work with a partner. Take turns to ask and answer questions using the words from this unit.

Writing

Write a letter to Grammarman and Tonic. Ask them questions about the grammar party tomorrow.

....
....
....
....
....
....
....
....
....
....
....

Present Perfect Simple: Regular and Irregular Verbs

Present Perfect Simple: Regular Verbs

Affirmative	Negative	Question
I have (I've) walked	I have not (haven't) walked	Have I walked?
you have (you've) walked	you have not (haven't) walked	Have you walked?
he has (he's) walked	he has not (hasn't) walked	Has he walked?
she has (she's) walked	she has not (hasn't) walked	Has she walked?
it has (it's) walked	it has not (hasn't) walked	Has it walked?
we have (we've) walked	we have not (haven't) walked	Have we walked?
you have (you've) walked	you have not (haven't) walked	Have you walked?
they have (they've) walked	they have not (haven't) walked	Have they walked?

Short answers

Yes, I have.	No, I haven't.
Yes, you have.	No, you haven't.
Yes, he has.	No, he hasn't.
Yes, she has.	No, she hasn't.
Yes, it has.	No, it hasn't.
Yes, we have.	No, we haven't.
Yes, you have.	No, you haven't.
Yes, they have.	No, they haven't.

We use the Present Perfect Simple to talk about:

- things that happened in the past, when we don't say when they happened. Sometimes we use the word *already*. We often use it to talk about our experiences.
  I have already eaten my lunch.
  I have visited lots of places in Italy.

- things which finished a short time ago. We often use the word *just*.
  The policemen have just left.
  I have just been to the shops.

- things that have not finished. We often use the word *yet*.
  She hasn't painted the doors yet.
  Has she painted the doors yet?

The Present Perfect Simple of regular verbs is formed with the auxiliary verb *have/has* and the past participle of the main verb. We form the past participle of regular verbs with the ending -ed, as we do for the Past Simple. The same spelling rules apply (see Unit 13).

We put the word *not* after the word *have/has* to make the negative form.
Graham has not cleaned his car this weekend.
They haven't posted the letters.

We put the word *have/has* before the subject to make the question form.
Has Jim prepared the food for the party?
Have you brushed your teeth?

---

1 Complete the sentences with the Present Perfect Simple.

Eg She *has finished* all her work. (finish)

1 Jim and Tonic ....
   lots of food for the party. (order)
2 I .... supper yet.
   (not cook)
3 They .... to three
   CDs this evening. (listen)
4 .... she .... her
   cousins three times this year? (visit)
5 You .... your room
   today. (not tidy)
6 My parents .... all
   over Europe. (travel)
7 We .... the shop.
   (close)
8 I .... here for five
   years. (live)

---

2 Complete the questions with the Present Perfect Simple and write answers.

Eg *Have you painted* your room? (you / paint) ✓
    Yes, I have.

1 .... at the hotel?
   (he / arrive) ✗
   ....

2 .... to do the
   exercises? (you / try) ✓
   ....

3 .... about the problem?
   (they / talk) ✗
   ....

4 .... the window?
   (she / open) ✗
   ....

5 .... playing?
   (the children / stop) ✓
   ....

6 .... this month?
   (it / rain) ✗
   ....

7 .... hard this year?
   (the students / study) ✓
   ....

8 .... the house?
   (Dad / clean) ✓
   ....

Present Perfect Simple: Irregular Verbs

The past participle of irregular verbs is not formed with the ending -ed. We form the past participle of these verbs in different ways. (See the Irregular Verbs list on page 108.)

do → did → done
find → found → found

Notes

The verb go has two past participles: gone and been.

We use have/has gone to say that someone has gone somewhere and has not come back yet.
Miriam has gone to the bank to get some money.

We use have/has been to say that someone went somewhere and has come back.
He has been to America.

3 Complete the chart.

Verb	Past Simple	Past Participle
be	was/were	*been*
come	came	
do	did	
draw	drew	
drink	drank	
eat	ate	
go	went	
have	had	
make	made	
sit	sat	
speak	spoke	
stand	stood	
take	took	
teach	taught	
write	wrote	

4 Complete the sentences with the Present Perfect Simple.

Eg I ...*haven't drunk*... all my coffee yet. (not drink)

1 Grammarman .... us lots of grammar! (teach)
2 We .... all the exercises. (do)
3 They .... all the chocolates. (not eat)
4 I .... my ring! (lose)
5 We .... miles today. (swim)
6 I .... any new clothes for a long time. (not buy)
7 .... Tonic .... a bowl of water? (drink)
8 We .... a wonderful time. (have)

5 Complete the questions with the Present Perfect Simple and write answers.

Eg ....*Have you been*........ to England? (you / go) ✗
........*No, I haven't.*........

1 .... her bag? (she / find) ✓
....

2 .... all their money? (they / spend) ✗
....

3 .... a hole for his bone? (Tonic / dig) ✓
....

4 .... the Eiffel Tower? (she / see) ✓
....

5 .... his parents before? (we / meet) ✗
....

6 .... all the irregular verbs? (you / learn) ✓
....

7 .... (the lesson / begin)? ✗
....

8 .... enough food? (they / buy) ✓
....

Look at the position of
already and yet in
the sentences.
I have already finished.
I haven't finished yet.

6 Write sentences with **already** and **yet**.

tidy my cupboards ✗   make my bed ✓
feed the dog ✓   wash the car ✗
do the shopping ✗   clean the kitchen ✓
go to the library ✗

Eg   *I haven't tidied my cupboards yet.*
     I have already fed the dog.

1   ....

2   ....

3   ....

4   ....

5   ....

Pairwork

Work with a partner. Take turns to ask and answer the
following questions:

- Have you visited any interesting places this year?
- Have you seen any good films this year?
- Have you read any good books this year?
- Have you learnt many new English words this year?
- Have you made any new friends this year?
- Have you been ill this year?
- Have you been to any birthday parties this year?

Writing

Write a short paragraph about this year. What have you done?
What haven't you done?

103

Review 5 (Units 17–20)

1 Complete the chart.

Adjective	Comparative	Superlative
tall	taller	the tallest
short		
small		
young		
light		
heavy		
easy		
big		
bad		
good		
hot		
interesting		
intelligent		
difficult		
comfortable		

2 Complete the sentences with **be going to** and the words in brackets.

Eg He .... *is going to take* .... his exam next Saturday. *(take)*

1 I .... a shower. (have)

2 They .... a new flat. (not buy)

3 We .... to a restaurant this evening. (not go)

4 It .... sunny tomorrow. (be)

5 We .... the match tomorrow! (win)

6 I .... for my exams tonight. (not study)

7 She .... a new pair of trainers. (not buy)

8 He .... his friends next week. (meet)

104

3

Complete the questions with **be going to** and write answers.

Eg ....*Is he going to send*........... me a postcard? *(he / send)* ✗
...............*No, he isn't.*...............

1 .... to the bus stop? *(you / run)* ✓
....

2 .... the piano for us this evening? *(she / play)* ✗
....

3 .... us tomorrow? *(they / ring)* ✓
....

4 .... to music all evening? *(he / listen)* ✗
....

5 .... all day? *(it / rain)* ✗
....

6 .... you soon? *(I / see)* ✓
....

7 .... at the station? *(we / meet)* ✓
....

8 .... the race? *(he / win)* ✗
....

4

Complete the sentences with the Future Simple.

Eg I ....*will be*................ very happy to see you. *(be)*

1 She .... at the same school next year. *(not be)*
2 We .... for you today. *(cook)*
3 .... they .... that again? *(do)*
4 I .... her to the party. *(not invite)*
5 Be good or you .... any cake! *(not have)*
6 I .... the door for you! *(open)*
7 They .... the presents with them when they visit us. *(bring)*
8 We .... late for lunch. *(not be)*

5

Complete the questions with the Future Simple and write answers.

Eg ....*Will it be*............... very hot tomorrow? *(it / be)* ✓
...............*Yes, it will.*...............

1 .... harder next year? *(you / try)* ✓
....

2 .... back early? *(he / get)* ✗
....

3 .... better tomorrow? *(she / feel)* ✓
....

4 .... me something from the shop? *(you / buy)* ✓
....

5 .... on the bus? *(they / be)* ✗
....

6 .... time to help us? *(he / have)* ✗
....

7 .... soon? *(you / write)* ✓
....

8 .... tired after their journey? *(they / be)* ✓
....

Choose the correct answer.

Eg   Who rode / did ride  *his bike down the road?*

1   Who *closed / did close* the window?
2   Who *did you write / you wrote* to?
3   What *did he see / he saw?*
4   What *smells / does smell* so nice?

5   Which car *you like / do you like* best?
6   Which jacket *costs / does cost* more?
7   Where *he went / did he go?*
8   Why *are you / you are* sad?

7   Complete the chart.

Verbs	Past Simple	Part Participle
buy	bought	*bought*
catch	caught	
dig	dug	
draw	drew	
drink	drank	
eat	ate	
go	went	
know	knew	
make	made	
sing	sang	
sit	sat	
speak	spoke	
spend	spent	
swim	swam	
take	took	
think	thought	

8
Complete the sentences with the correct form of the Present Perfect Simple.

Eg   I ......*have lost*...... *my keys again! (lose)*

1   He .... miles today! (run)
2   I .... any food from the supermarket. (not buy)
3   The cat .... a bowl of milk. (drink)
4   We .... a lovely time! (have)
5   She .... her brother recently. (not see)
6   .... they .... a letter to their cousins? (write)
7   I .... all my jobs for today! (do)
8   They .... in the sea. (swim)

9 Write the sentences and questions with the Present Perfect Simple.

Eg   I / not listen / to my new CD / yet
    I haven't listened to my new CD yet.

1   you / not clean / your room / yet
    ....

2   my parents / visit / a lot of places
    ....

3   we / already finish /our meal
    ....

4   I / not live / here / for long
    ....

5   Tonic / always be / a clever dog / ?
    ....

6   they / ask /about the party / ?
    ....

10 Complete the questions with the Present Perfect Simple and write answers.

Eg   ....*Have you counted*.................... the money? (you / count) ✓
    ....*Yes, I have.*....................

1   .... Italy? (you / visit) ✗
    ....

2   .... her keys? (she / find) ✓
    ....

3   .... a new motorbike?
    (he / buy) ✗
    ....

4   Where is Rosie? .... to
    her friend's house? (she / go) ✓
    ....

5   .... that film? (you / see) ✓
    ....

6   .... in England? (he / arrive) ✗
    ....

7   .... your house? (you /
    sell) ✓
    ....

8   .... about the problem?
    (they / talk) ✗
    ....

11 Choose the correct answer.

Eg   *Has the lesson* began / (begun)?

1   They didn't *bought / buy* any nice clothes.

2   Have you *meet / met* his wife?

3   They *haven't / didn't* clean the house today.

4   Does he *teach / taught* at your school?

5   She *have / has* driven miles today!

6   She *came / come* to the party last night.

7   Have you *flew / flown* in an aeroplane?

8   I *broke / broken* two glasses this week.

Irregular verbs

Infinitive	Past Simple	Past Participle	Infinitive	Past Simple	Past Participle
be	was/were	been	lead	led	led
become	became	become	learn	learnt (learned)	learnt (learned)
begin	began	begun	leave	left	left
blow	blew	blown	lend	lent	lent
break	broke	broken	lose	lost	lost
bring	brought	brought	make	made	made
build	built	built	meet	met	met
buy	bought	bought	pay	paid	paid
catch	caught	caught	put	put	put
choose	chose	chosen	read	read	read
come	came	come	ride	rode	ridden
cut	cut	cut	ring	rang	rung
do	did	done	run	ran	run
draw	drew	drawn	say	said	said
drink	drank	drunk	see	saw	seen
drive	drove	driven	sell	sold	sold
eat	ate	eaten	shine	shone	shone
fall	fell	fallen	sing	sang	sung
feed	fed	fed	sit	sat	sat
feel	felt	felt	sleep	slept	slept
find	found	found	speak	spoke	spoken
fly	flew	flown	spend	spent	spent
forget	forgot	forgotten	stand	stood	stood
get	got	got	swim	swam	swum
give	gave	given	take	took	taken
go	went	gone	teach	taught	taught
grow	grew	grown	tell	told	told
have	had	had	think	thought	thought
hear	heard	heard	understand	understood	understood
hit	hit	hit	wake	woke	woken
hurt	hurt	hurt	wear	wore	worn
keep	kept	kept	win	won	won
know	knew	known	write	wrote	written

Notes

Notes

Notes